The Allure of
TOY SHIPS

American & European nautical toys from
the 19th and 20th centuries

ANTIQUE
COLLECTORS'
CLUB

The Allure of
TOY SHIPS

American & European nautical toys from
the 19th and 20th centuries

by Richard T. Claus

To Dottie
Who put up with all this!

———————

ISBN 1-85149-501-0

British Library Cataloguing-in-Publication Data
A catalogue record for this book is available from
the British Library

Photography: Richard T. Claus
Graphic Design: Joel J. Weissman

Printed in China
for the Antique Collectors' Club Ltd., Sandy Lane,
Old Martlesham, Woodbridge, Suffolk IP12 4SD, UK

Contents

Note: An index of individual manufacturers may be found
on the introductory pages of their respective countries.

Arnold, Co.

see page 67

Foreword

The hundred year period between 1850 and 1950 was the golden age of ship development. Ships evolved from sail and wood to steam and steel. The industrial revolution was in full swing, changing forever our way of life. Nations of the world depended on their ships for national protection and colonial trade. The powerful dreadnoughts and massive ocean liners of the early 20th century were national symbols and as fascinating to children then as are space shuttles today. As toys imitate real life, those made in European and American factories were sometimes accurate representations and sometimes not, but they all followed the interests of children in an evolving mechanized society. As focus shifted to automobiles and then to aircraft, interest in ships waned. Reflecting current tastes, toy catalogs of the period slowly but surely devoted less and less space to ships. By the 1950's they had become a small segment of the toy market, yet they remain today as a testament to their times.

While I have been a toy railroad enthusiast from childhood, about 30 years ago a combined interest in toys, transportation, history, and the sea drew me toward toy ships. Although toy boats were available in the antique market, their relative rarity made acquisition a risky issue, especially since adequate knowledge regarding the pieces was spotty. Fortunately, about that time several books came on the market, which gave me a starting point and some incentive. In spite of my new enthusiasm, it was a difficult learning curve. There was a lot of misinformation to overcome, both in print and otherwise.

Another problem was that since toy ships were by their very nature used in an environment unfriendly toward tinplate, they were more often than not found in a deteriorated state. It was difficult to determine what a piece looked like when new or if it had been repaired, let alone who had made it! Apparently I was in good company, for the experts of the day were no more knowledgeable than I. Thus began a long struggle to piece together a collection that I could definitively and accurately describe. My emphasis was to focus on condition and originality.

When reading this book several points should be considered:

Only toy ships formerly or currently in the RTC collection are described in the book. No attempt was made to include every toy ship manufacturer, yet there was an effort to collect a variety of makers. The author's preferences obviously influenced the ships chosen. The pieces illustrated have been personally inspected, measured and cataloged.

The knowledgeable toy collector knows as much, if not more, about specific manufacturers as the author, so only a brief listing, as a matter of perspective, is offered. Selections for further reading can be found in the Bibliography and Related Reading section.

Ship measurements are for actual hull length to the nearest 1/8 inch. This does not include extensions such as rudder or bowsprit. Numbers in brackets, i.e. (M-31), are inventory numbers, which are the key to the price estimates index. Prices are for toys of condition 8+ or higher.

While care was taken to be accurate, dates should be considered as approximate. Production was almost always carried out over an extended period of time.

I do not presume to make this book the oracle of toy ships. Mistakes are inevitable. I do hope, however, that *The Allure of Toy Ships* will be a starting point for ever-expanding information regarding the fascinating hobby of collecting these wonderful toys.

Richard T. Claus

American Manufacturers

(AB-1) 1874, 13″ clockwork steamboat No. 50½ *Plymouth Rock*. This floor toy has a profile quite similar to those of George Brown. Brown's, however, did not have the stern steering wheels.

2

AB-1

NAME	LOCATION	DATES	FOUNDER	PAGE
Althof-Bergmann	New York, NY	1867-1880	3 Bergman Bros. & L. Althof	2
American Toyland Creators	Brooklyn, NY	–	–	10
Artwood Toy Mfg. Co.	New York, NY	1930's-1940's	–	3
Baker & Bennett	–	–	–	3
Bliss, R., Mfg. Co.	Pawtucket, RI	1832-1914	Rufus Bliss	3
Boucher, H.E., Mfg. Co.	New York, NY	1905-1950's	H. E. Boucher	4
Bramwell-Smith	–	–	–	4
Brown, George	Forestville, CT	1856-1880	George Brown	5
Cappel & MacDonald	Dayton, OH	1930's-1940's		6
Cass, N.D., Co.	Athol, MA	1890's-?	–	6
Chein, J., & Co.	New York, NY	1903-1979	Julius Chein	7
Cohn, T., Inc.	Brooklyn, NY	–	–	8
Consolidated Toy Mfg. Co.	Lawrence, MA	–	–	8
Converse, Morton E., Co.	Winchendon, MA	1878-1934	Morton Converse	9
Dent Hardware Co.	Fullerton, PA	1895-1937	Henry H. Dent	8
Fallows, James, & Sons	Philadelphia, PA	1870-?	James Fallows	10
Gilbert, A.C., Co.	New Haven, CT	1913-1966	A.C.Gilbert	10
Gobar Mfg. Co.	Elkhart, IN	–		10
Ideal Novelty & Toy Co.	Brooklyn, NY	1903-?	Rose & Morris Michtom	10
Ives Mfg. Co.	Bridgeport, CT	1868-1932	Edward R. Ives	11-15
Keystone Mfg. Co.	Boston, MA	1920-1956/7	Marx Bros.	16-19
Keystone Wood Toys	Boston, MA	1934-1957	–	16-19
Liberty Playthings, Inc.	East Aurora, NY	1928-1932	George Moore	20
Lindstrom Tool & Toy Co.	Bridgeport, CT	1913?-193?	F.L. Lindstrom	20-21
Lionel Corp.	New York, NY	1900-?	Lionel Cowan	22

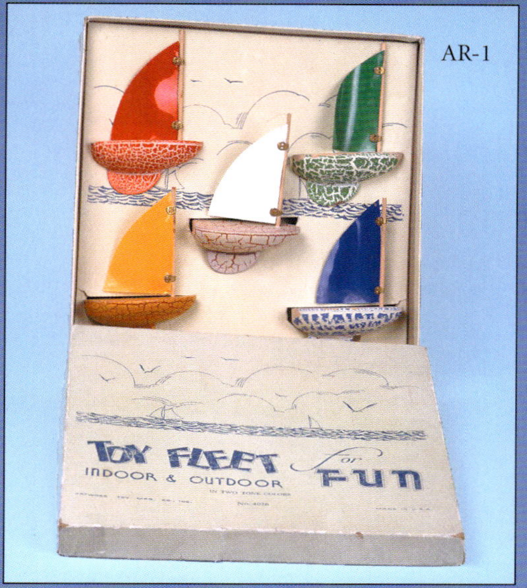

AR-1

BL-1

R. Bliss, Mfg. Co.

(BL-1) 1895, 18″ *HMS Blake.* This ship was replaced in the 1896 Bliss catalog by a similar one named *Conqueror.* It had a retail price of 25 cents! The real *HMS Blake* was one of two in the Blenheim class of 20-knot British cruisers. It visited the US in 1893 being only three years old at the time. It was still in service in 1906.

Artwood Toy Mfg. Co.

(AR-1) 1930-40's, 3″. One can only imagine how this fragile fleet would have survived without the protection of its original box!

Baker & Bennett

Rear: (UK-5) 1906-1918, 14″ wooden battleship with cannon. The unknown manufacturer must not have been aware of the "King's English" spelling for the revolutionary British battleship of 1906, *HMS Dreadnought.*
Front: (BB-1) 1910, 12″ exploding wooden battleship. Schoenhut and Keystone provided variants on this theme.

UK-5

BB-1

NAME	LOCATION	DATES	FOUNDER	PAGE
Marx, Louis, & Co.	New York, NY	1919-1973	Louis Marx	22
Mengel Co., Inc.	St. Louis, MO	–	–	23
M&P Co. (Roll-O-Float)	–	–	–	23
Ny-Cal Co., The	Whittier, CA	–	–	22
Ohio Art Co.	Bryan, OH	1908 to date	Henry Winzeler	23
Orkin, Samuel, Co.	Cambridge, MA	1916-1930	Samuel Orkin	24-26
Orkincraft (Calwis Ind. Ltd.)	Beverly Hills, CA	1930-1934	–	26
Reed, W.S., Toy Co.	Leominster, MA	1875-1894	–	27
Robin Mfg. Co.	–	–	–	27
Schieble Toy & Novelty Co.	Dayton, OH	1909-1931	Wm. Schieble/D.P. Clark (1898)	28-29
Schoenhut	Philadelphia, PA	1872-1935	Albert Schoenhut	30
Skipper Mfg. Co	Chicago, IL	1930's-50's	–	30
Strauss, Ferdinand, Corp.	New York, NY	1904-1942	Ferdinand Strauss	31
Strombeck-Becker Mfg. Co	Moline, IL	1930's-50's	1961 bought by Dowst	31
Tillicum Sales Co.	Tacoma WA	1920's-30's	acquired by Milton Bradley	32-33
Tillicum / Milton Bradley	Springfield, MA	1860 to date	Milton Bradley	33-34
Tootsietoy (Dowst Mfg.Co.)	Chicago, IL	1890's-?	C.O. & S. Dowst	35
Transogram Co,	New York, NY	–	–	35
Tudor Button & Novelty Co.	–	–	–	35
Union Mfg. Co.	Clinton, CT	1853 -1869	bought by Hull & Stratford	36
Unknown	Various	–	–	36
Walbert Mfg. Co.	Chicago, IL	?-1927	acquired by Wolverine	36
Weeden Mfg.Co.	New Bedford, MA	1883-195?	Wm.N. Weeden	37
Wilkins / Kingsbury	Keene, NH	1890-1942	J.S. Wilkins / H.T. Kingsbury	37
Wolverine Supply & Mfg. Co.	Pittsburgh, PA	1903-1950's	Mr. & Mrs. Benjamin F. Bains	38-39
Wyandotte Toys	Wyandotte, MI	1921-1956	G. Stallings & W.F. Schmidt	39

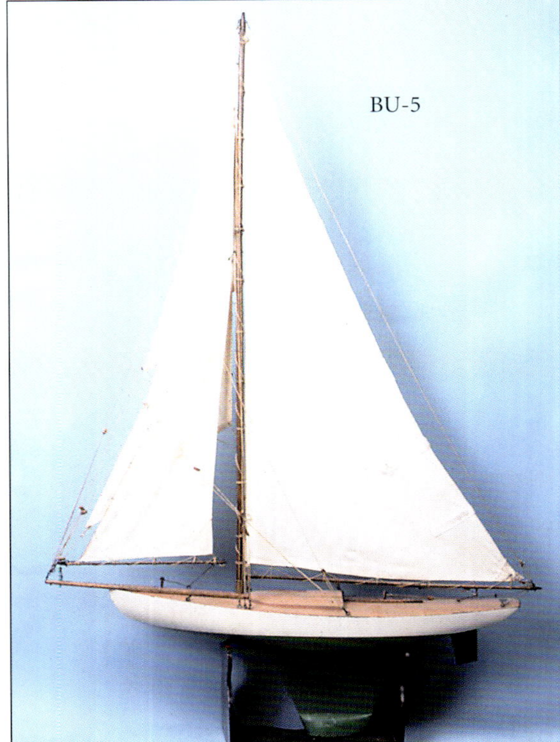

BU-5

H.E. Boucher Mfg. Co.

(BU-5) **1928, 25″**
Coot came ready to sail.
Hull is made of "Patented
Composition" and Boucher
literature also claims
a "Patented Sail
Shifting Device."

Top: (BU-3) **1920's metal
22″ speedboat** *Polly-Wog.*
Bottom: (BU-1) **1920's wooden
clockwork 24″ speedboat**
Minnow. This boat also came
as a construction set.

4

Bramwell-Smith

(BS-1) **10 ¹⁄₂″ paddle-wheeler, patent date
1872.** It has a cleverly designed spirit fired
system which uses a double hull section for
fuel storage. The entire steam plant/paddle
wheel mechanism can be removed by simply
rotating one hold-down lever.

(BR-2) 1870, 20″. Shown in the *George Brown Toy Sketchbook,* this boat bears a striking similarity to one produced by Rock and Graner in Wurttemberg. Except for the paint scheme, the comparative dimensions are so much the same that it is almost certain that the Brown boat was either made in Germany or that it was copied from the Rock & Graner boat.

Top: (BR-3) 1870, 33″. Bottom: (BR-2) 1870, 20″ #7. Both are clockwork. The large paddle-wheeler in the background is not shown in a George Brown catalog, but is quite similar in design and color to the boat in front. It could also be German.

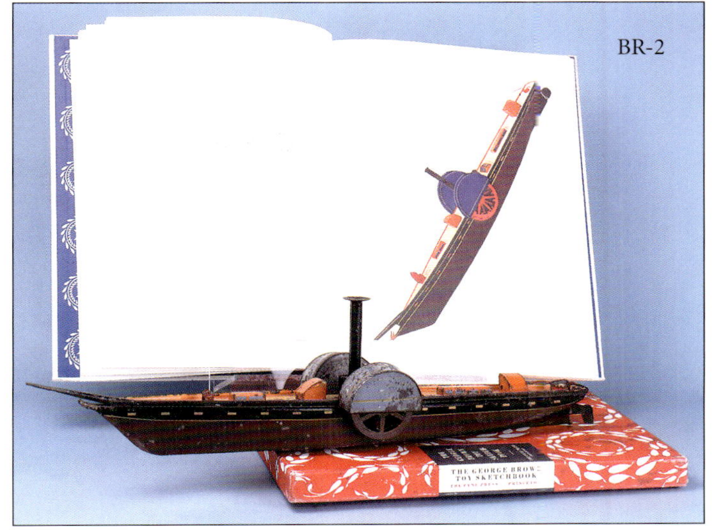

(BR-5) 1870, 7″ #6 *Victory.* This is the smallest George Brown clockwork boat. A larger version was 14″. Rumor has it that Bill Holland would produce this boat from his pocket at flea markets to the awe of all present and claim it as a recent find.

(BR-1) 1872, 14″ #28, *Monitor* was shown in the Stevens & Brown catalog of 1872 as a clockwork toy. The version here is a pull toy offered in the 1874 Althof-Bergmann catalog as No. 509.

(CM-1) 1930's.
One of many wooden boat block construction sets available for the budding naval architect during the 20th Century.

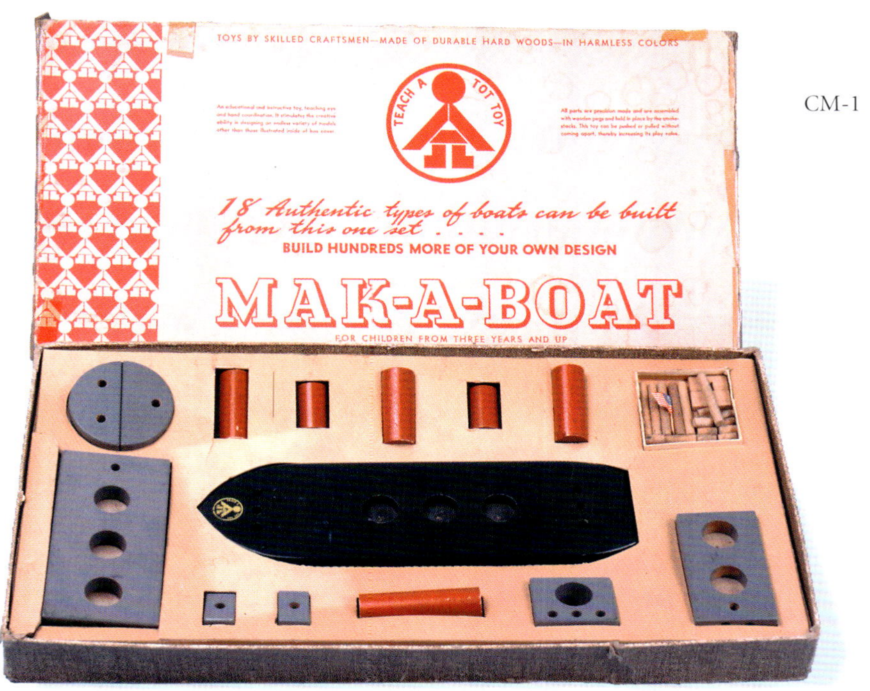

CM-1

These Cass wooden boats were made in the 1940's and 50's.
Clockwise from the upper left:
(CS-2) 16″ sailboat,
(CS-3) 8″ tug,
(CS-1) 12″ liner,
(CS-4) 16″ liner.
None are powered.

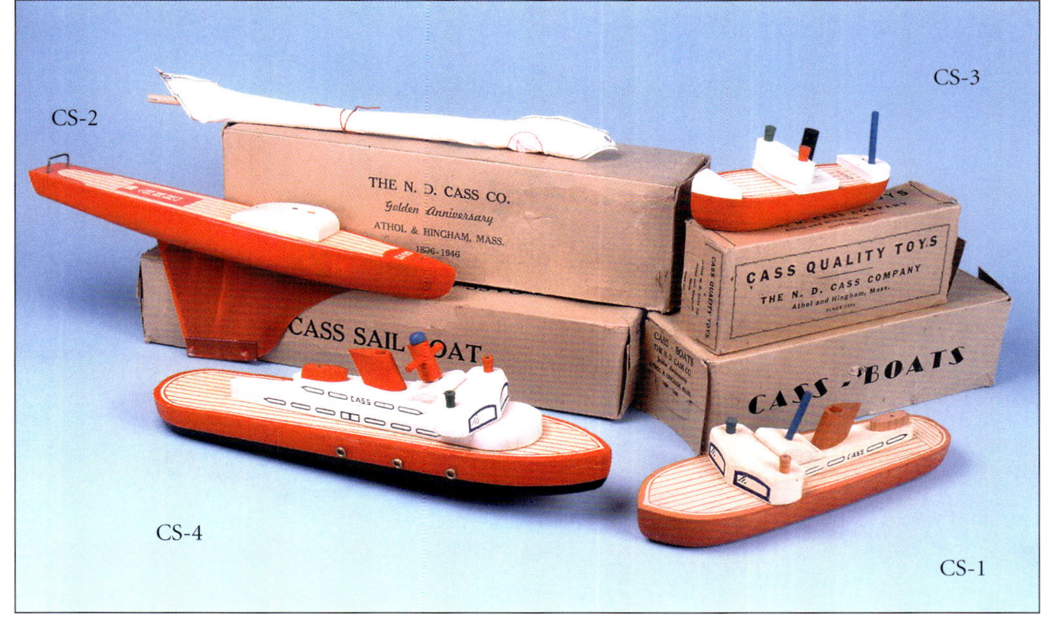

Clockwise from rear: (CH-3) 1950, 14″ #126 *Peggy Jane* motorboat; (CH-1) 1920's, 10″ *Emma* motorboat; (CH-2) 1960, 8″ #106 motorboat. From the 1920's into the 1960's any number of inexpensive clockwork boats were produced.

Both sailboats are from the 1930's. In the rear is Chein's largest ship, (CH-4) 23″ #1500, *Peggy Jane.* Its diminutive sister (CH-5) 12″ #711 *Peggy Ann* is in the foreground.

Left to right: (CH-6), (CH-7). Made from the 1930's into the 1950's, above are two versions of the 7″ clockwork #56 motor boat.

Complete with plastic sails, these two wooden sailboats are from the 1960's. Left to right: (CD-1) 8″ *Patti Ann*, (CD-2) 11″ *Flying Cloud.*

CD-1   CD-2

(DT-1) 1899, 20″ #8 cruiser *New York.* Showing how toys reflect their times, this large cast iron floor toy was issued to take advantage of the euphoria surrounding Adm. William T. Sampson's victory in Santiago July 3, 1898. Although he was not present until the end of the battle, the belted cruiser, completed in 1893, was his flagship.

DT-1

Left to right: (CN-3) 10″ #15 sand toy; (CN-1) 7″ ea., set of five motorboats, only one is clockwork powered; (CN-2) 14″ clockwork motorboat. All are from 1950 -1960.

This was a set shown in the October 26th, 1899 issue of *The Youth's Companion* as one of the premiums for selling subscriptions to the magazine.
Back: (CE-4) 14″ *Reliance*.
Front, left to right:
(CE-2) 17″ pull toy battleship *New York*,
(CE-1) 7″ clockwork steamer *Three Friends*. The little steamer is wound by rotating its stack.

Steel hulled sailboats made between 1895 and 1927. Called "Improved Steel Yachts" and cataloged as Line #900, they came in 8 sizes, every two inches, from 10″ to 24″. Their hulls can be found in three colors: red, blue or green. All seem to be named after successful America's Cup participants, such as *Defender, Columbia, Reliance and Resolute*. A folding keel feature found on some was patented in 1903.
Clockwise from rear:
(CE-6) 18″ *Resolute*,
(CE-4) 14″ *Reliance*,
(CE-9) 12″ *Columbia*,
(CE-7) 16″ *Resolute*,
(CE-5) 20″ *Columbia*.

Pictured are two versions of the 1870 12″ *Columbia*. Top: (FS-1) clockwork. Bottom: (FS-2) pull toy. Both have the cryptic Fallows "IXL" trademark embossed on the deck under the pilothouse.

(ID-1) 1918, 11″ steam powered submarine. As art imitates life, the idea of a steam powered sub is not as bizarre as it sounds. The Royal Navy had an entire flotilla of steam propelled submarines during WW I. They proved to be quite unreliable and dangerous. This toy boat is only a surface runner.

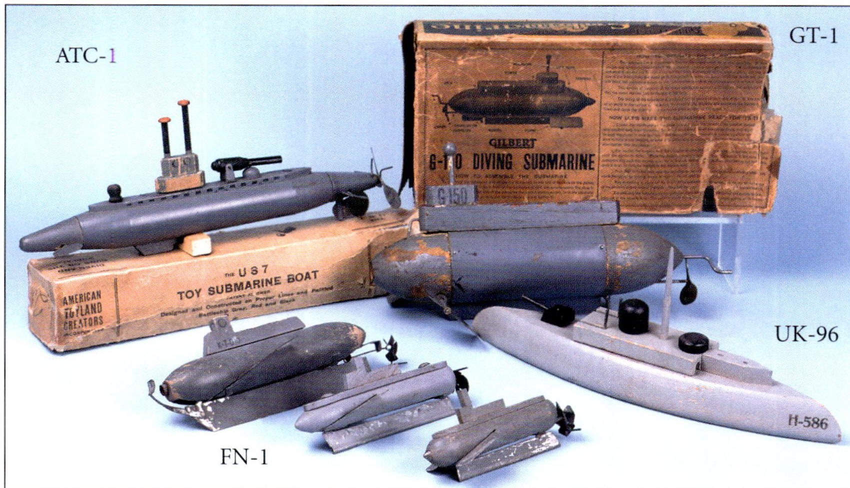

This gaggle of wooden subs is from the 1910's and 1920's. Clockwise from the left rear: (ATC-1) American Toyland Creators, 13″ rubber band powered; (GT-1) Gilbert, 11″ rubber band powered; (UK-96) Keystone?, 14″ nonpowered; (FN-1) Fulton?, 5″, 6″ *and* 8″ rubber band powered.

(GB-1) 1930, 9″ put-put speedboat. Literally thousands of this toy were sold and are still often seen for sale at shows.

(I-21) **1869, 11″ clockwork single oarsman, *U.S.Grant.* An elongated version of this boat came as a double oarsman.**

I-21

Although Ives made clockwork and steam driven toy boats in the latter part of the 19th Century, their greatest foray into the nautical field occurred in 1918 and lasted until 1927. Ives apparently perceived an opening in the U.S market with the advent of the First World War in 1914. Subsequent lack of imports from Germany reinforced this idea and they announced their new boat line in December of 1917. War driven shortages delayed shipments until late 1918 or early 1919.

A review of trade advertisements in *Playthings* reveals that while boats were cataloged until 1927, Ives discontinued their promotional efforts to dealers after 1924.

In all, there were seven types of tin boats (freighters, subs, etc.). Certain boats lasted from their introduction, with modifications, until 1927. Others were totally redesigned in 1922. Since we can cover the entire period of manufacture in only ten years, the following chart (pg.15) can be most useful in identifying early versions from late. I have separated the production period into 1st Series (1918-1921 and for some 1927) and 2nd Series (1922-1927). While 1st Series boats have many minor variations, two major variations exist for all and three for some. These major variations are listed chronologically as A, B and C. On the other hand, 2nd Series boats seem to be quite uniform.

In 1922, Ives introduced a line of sailboats. These wooden hulled ships came either as kits or finished. There were four cataloged numbers with four different rigs. All utilized the same 30 inch hull. The Ives booklet was revised to reflect this new type to: *Yachting, Ships and Shipping.*

There is little doubt that, as production advanced from year to year, some overlapping of characteristics occurred. Thus, we might find rubber stamping on the hull bottom and a name on the bow. Or we might find cotter pin handrails and a removable motor. In general, however, the older and newer features are as stated.

The earliest printing of the Ives booklet, *Ships and Shipping*, lists an 18 inch and a 24 inch size for all types except the sub and tug. Although examples of these reportedly exist, it is doubtful that they were ever produced. I have never seen one in my thirty years of collecting, nor did Ives mention these sizes in their ads to the trade. Their catalog numbers are not included on the chart

Because of the lack of metal preparation and the use of shiny tinplate, the paint on Ives boats today is more often than not quite distressed. Finding good examples can therefore be quite a challenge.

11

Submarines

Top to bottom: (I-2) 10½″ #1009 Series 1A,
(I-30) 10½″ #1009 Series 1B, (I-1) 10½″ #1009 Series
1C. **The top two boats are missing their periscopes,
a common problem.**

Tugs

Top to bottom: (I-9) 10½″ #2010 Series 2,
(I-11) 9″ #2009 Series 1A, (I-29) 9″ #2009 Series 1B.

Destroyers

Top to bottom: (I-14) 9″ #3009 Series 1B,
(I-36) 9″ #3009 Series 1A, (I-13) 9″ #3009 Series 1C.

Destroyers

Top to bottom: (I-12) 12″ #3012 Series 1B,
(I-32) 12″ #3012 Series 1A, (I-22) 12″ #3012 Series 1C.

Motor Boats
Top to bottom:
(I-8) 9″ #4009 Series 1A, (I-7) 9″ #4009 Series 1B,
(I-34) 12″ #4012 Series 1A, (I-6) 12″ #4012 Series 1B.

Scout Patrol Boats
Left to right: (I-3) 12″ #4013 Series 1B,
(I-23) 9″ #4010 Series 1B.

Scout Patrol Boats
Left to right: (I-5) 13½″ #4014 Series 2
(I-31) 10½″ #4011 Series 2.

Scout Patrol Boats
Left to right: (I-4) 12″ #4013 Series 1A,
(I-28) 9″ #4010 Series 1A.

Freighters
Top to bottom:
(I-16) 10½″ #6011 Series 2,
(I-15) 13½″ #6014 Series 2.

Freighters
Top to bottom: (I-17) 12″ #6012 Series 1B,
(I-18) 9″ #6009 Series 1A, (I-19) 9″ #6009 Series 1B.

Ocean Liners
Top to bottom: (I-25) 13½″ #5014 Series 2,
(I-33) 10½″ #5011 Series 2.

Ocean Liners
Top to bottom: (I-26) 12″ #5012 Series 1B,
(I-27) 9″ #5009 Series 1B, (I-35) 12″ #5012 Series 1A.

(I-20) 1870's, 9″ steam powered yacht #326. This is one of three hull sizes and was available in brass or painted tin.

I-20

IVES SHIPS

RTC #	IVES #	SERIES	DESCRIPTION	IVES LENGTH	YEARS # WAS CATALOGUED	COMMENTS
I-2	1009	1A	Submarine	10$\frac{1}{2}$″	1918-1925	Cotter Pin & Wire Handrail, Med. Grey
I-30	1009	1B	Submarine	10$\frac{1}{2}$″	–	Stamped Handrail, Med. Grey
I-1	1009	1C	Submarine	10$\frac{1}{2}$″	–	No Hand Rail, Dark Grey
I-11	2009	1A	Tug Boat	9″	1918-1921	"Tug Boat" on Bottom, no Bow Name, one Mast
I-29	2009	1B	Tug Boat	9″	–	"King" on Bow, two Masts
I-9	2010	2	Tug Boat	10$\frac{1}{2}$″	1922-1927	"King" on Bow
I-36	3009	1A	Destroyer	9″	1918-1927	Dot Portholes, "Destroyer" on Bottom
I-14	3009	1B	Destroyer	9″	–	"3009"
I-13	3009	1C	Destroyer	9″	–	"3009", Uses 4009B Deck w/Inset
I-32	3012	1A	Destroyer	12″	1918-1927	–
I-12	3012	1B	Destroyer	12″	–	"3012"
I-22	3012	1C	Destroyer	12″	–	"3012", Uses 4012B Deck w/Inset
I-8	4009	1A	Motor Boat	9″	1918-1927	"Motor Boat" on Bottom, no Bow Name
I-7	4009	1B	Motor Boat	9″	–	"Vim" on Bow
I-28	4010	1A	Scout Patrol	9″	1918-1921	"Scout Patrol" on Bow, "O" Portoles
I-23	4010	1B	Scout Patrol	9″	–	"Sally" on Bow
I-31	4011	2	Scout Patrol	10$\frac{1}{2}$″	1922-1927	"Sally" on Bow
I-34	4012	1A	Motor Boat	12″	1918-1927	"Motor Boat" on Bottom, no Bow Name
I-6	4012	1B	Motor Boat	12″	–	"Vixen" on Bow
I-4	4013	1A	Scout Patrol	12″	1918-1921	"Scout Patrol" on Bottom, no Bow Name
I-3	4013	1B	Scout Patrol	12″	–	"Roamer" on Bow
I-5	4014	2	Scout Patrol	13$\frac{1}{2}$″	1922-1927	"Roamer" on Bow
–	5009	1A	Ocean Liner	9″	1918-1921	"Ocean Liner" on Bottom, "O" Portholes, no Name
I-27	5009	1B	Ocean Liner	9″	–	"Chicago" on Bow
I-33	5011	2	Ocean Liner	10$\frac{1}{2}$″	1922-1927	"Chicago" on Bow
I-35	5012	1A	Ocean Liner	12″	1918-1921	"Ocean Liner" on Bottom, "O" Portholes, no Name
I-26	5012	1B	Ocean Liner	12″	–	"New York" on Bow
I-25	5014	2	Ocean Liner	13$\frac{1}{2}$″	1922-1927	"New York" on Bow
I-18	6009	1A	Merchant Marine	9″	1918-1921	"U.S. Merchant Marine" on Bow, Dot Portholes
I-19	6009	1B	Merchant Marine	9″	–	"U.S. Merchant Marine" on Bow
I-16	6011	2	Merchant Marine	10$\frac{1}{2}$″	1922-1927	"U.S. Merchant Marine" on Bow
–	6012	1A	Merchant Marine	12″	1918-1921	"U.S. Merchant Marine" on Bow, Dot Portholes
I-17	6012	1B	Merchant Marine	12″	–	"U.S. Merchant Marine" on Bow
I-15	6014	2	Merchant Marine	13$\frac{1}{2}$″	1922-1927	"U.S. Merchant Marine" on Bow

Features of 1st Series (1918) Early Type (A):
Name on bottom of hull when not named on Bow.
(Motor Boat, Ocean Liner, etc.)
Zero ("0") or Dot used for Portholes
Non-Removable Clockwork Motors
Tabbed Motor Access Hatch
Short (relative to later models) Stacks
Cotter Pin & Wire Handrails

Features of 1st Series Later Type (B):
Names on Bow
Portholes are Circular with Central Dot
Removable Motor
Motor Access Hatches are Cabins & Lift Off (untabbed) or Pry Out like Cocoa Can Lids
Stamped Handrails

2nd Series (1922-1927):
Hulls & Upperworks completely redesigned for:
Tug, Scout Patrol (2 sizes), Ocean Liner (2 sizes) and Merchant Marine (2 sizes)

(K-24) Not often found, let alone in its original box, this wonderful wooden set was sold in the late 1940's and early 50's.

K-24

16

(K-10) 23″. Driven by a powerful clockwork motor, this ocean liner was the queen of the 1930's Keystone wooden boat line.

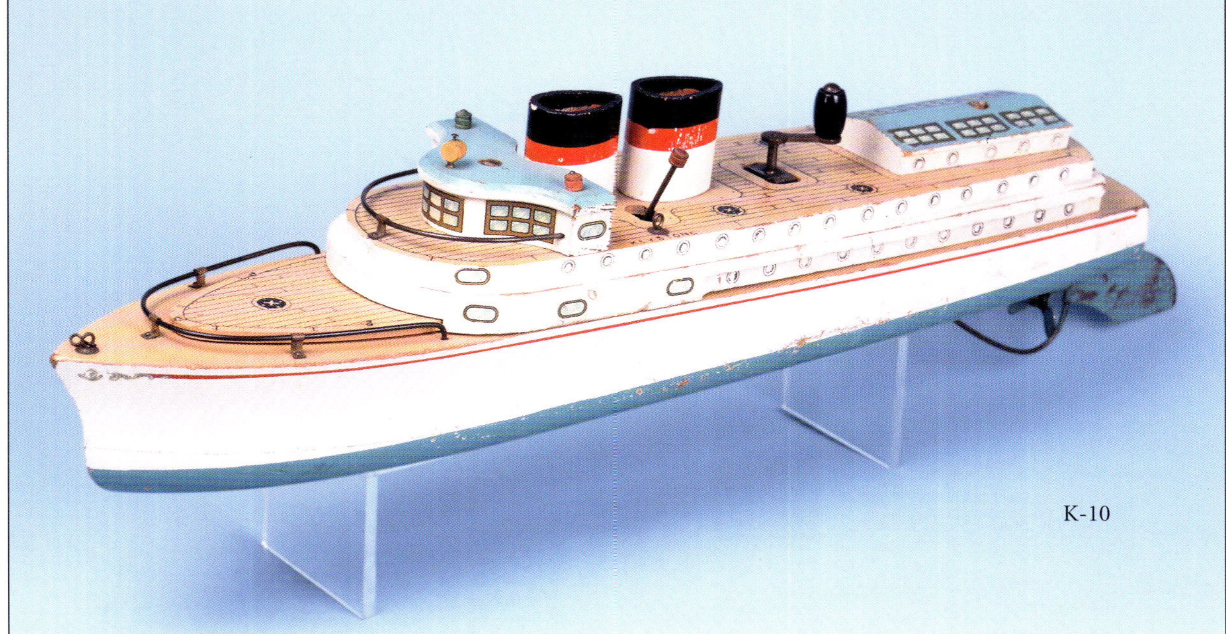

K-10

Summer Dreams: Fishing, Sailing, and Speedboat Racing. (K18) 11″ fishing boat with pole & fish, (K-12) 15″ #319 sailboat, (K16) 12″ clockwork powered speedboat. All are wooden.

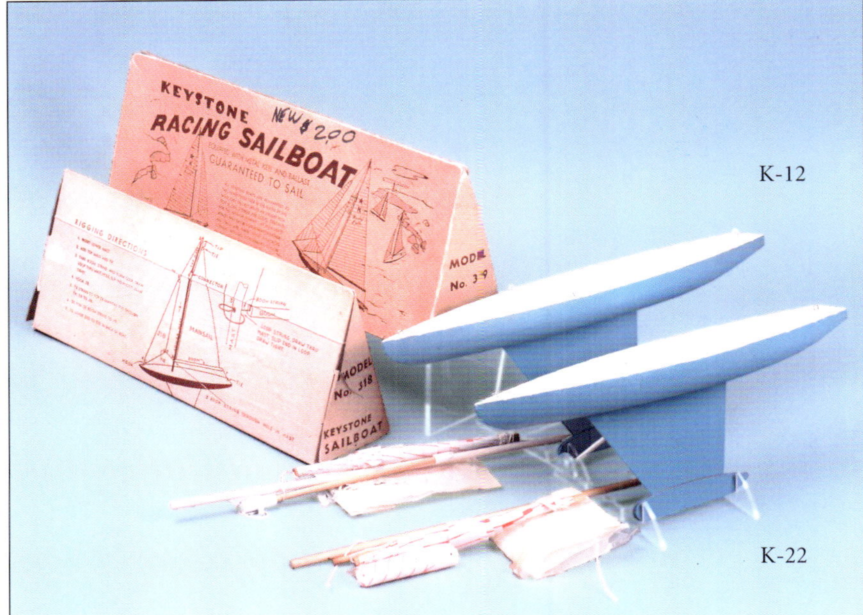

Wooden Sailboats
(K-25) *Tub–n–Table Fleet* from the 1930's.

Wooden Sailboats
Left to right: (K-12) 15″ #319 and
(K-22) 14″ #318, from the 1940-50 era.

Wooden Warships
Back: (K-13) 14″ aircraft carrier (single plane version).
Front, left to right: (K-3) 14″ rocket ship,
(K-5) 14″ sub with rubber band powered torpedo,
(K-15) 11″ submarine, (K-14) 14″ cruiser.

Popular during WW II, warships ruled the Keystone wooden fleet. Clockwise from the left: (K-21) 13″ #251 radar rocket ship, (K-4) 15″ #215 battleship, (K-1) 15″ aircraft carrier, (K-11) 13″ #255 radar rocket ship, (K-2) 13″ battle fleet. This is an updated version of the 1915 Schoenhut submarine and exploding battleship.

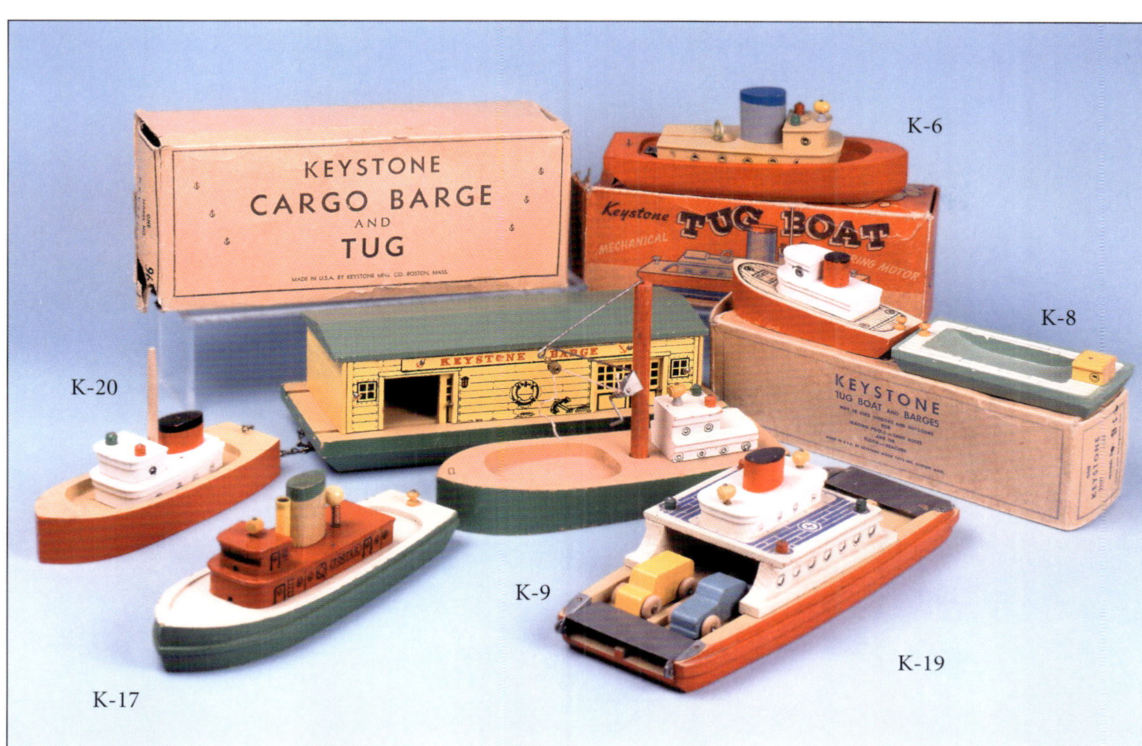

Shown is a sampling of the variety of wooden harbor craft made during the 1940's and 50's. Clockwise from left rear: (K-20) #967 cargo barge and its 7″ tug, (K-6) 9″ clockwork powered tug, (K-8) #314 6″ tug with barge, (K-19) 12″ ferry, (K-9) 10″ lighter with crane, (K-17) 9″ tug with whistle.

Top: (K-23) 18″. Bottom: (K-7) 8″. Both wooden boats are from the 1930's and are powered by electric motors.

(UK-27) 1930's, 18″ clockwork wooden stern-wheeler. Although the manufacturer cannot be positively stated, this unusual toy has all the hallmarks of Keystone.

(LY-6) **1929, 28″ aircraft carrier.** This wooden ship has a clockwork motor and the wheels are removable for sea duty. Aircraft (not original) are stored in a compartment below the hinged deck.

1928-1932. Rear: (LY-1) 22″ fireboat. Middle: (LY-4) 15″ cabin cruiser. Front, left to right: (LY-5) 12″ tug, (LY-2) 12″ sea scooter. All have clockwork motors and wooden hulls.

20

In 1931, possibly to boost sales with a lower priced product, wooden boats with mechanical motors were introduced. Clockwise from left rear: (UK-54) and (UK-101) **12″ speedboats** (Keystone ?), (L-12) **15″ cabin cruiser** with outboard motor, (UK-29) **10″** and (UK-53) **7″ rubber band powered speedboats** (Keystone ?), (L-10) **10″ outboard hydroplane,** (L-11) **8″ two-man outboard sea sled,** (L-9) **10″ No. 250 rowboat and outboard.**

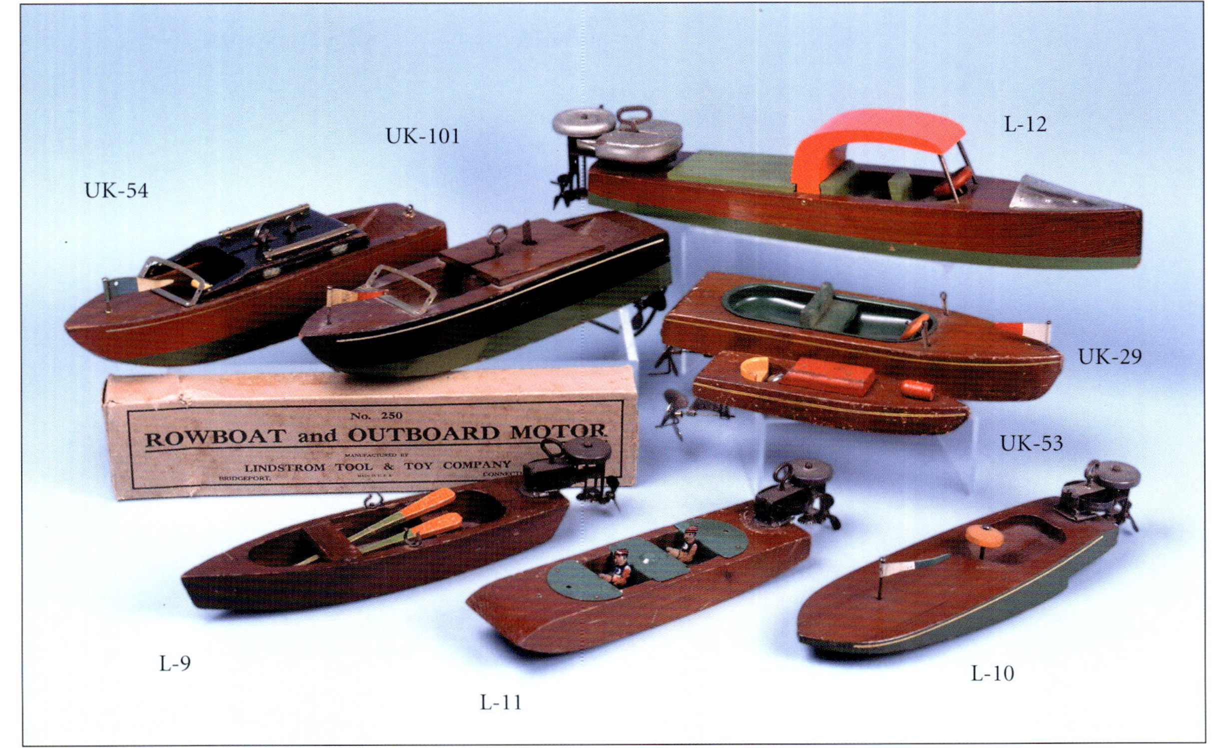

1920's and 1930's tin clockwork boats.
Clockwise from left front: (L-7) 7″ PT 10, (L-8) 13″ liner,
(L-2) 14″ #173 liner, (L-5) 14″ #135 speedboat,
(L-4) 10″ *Baby L*, (L-3) 10″ *Baby Wee*, (L-14) 7″ *The Define 7*,
(L-6) 10″ outboard speedboat, large outboard motor.

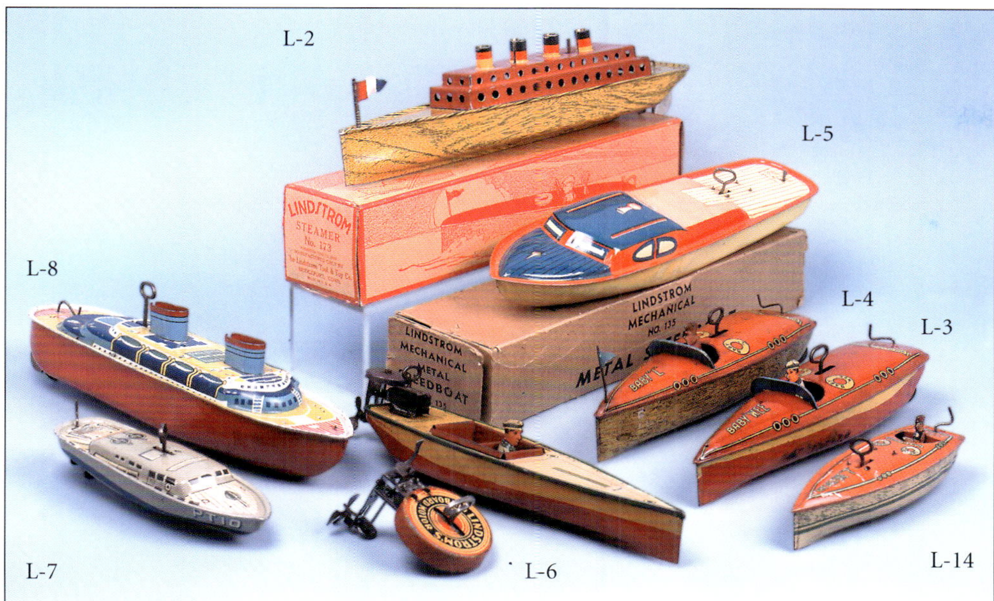

(L-15) 1920's, 18″ clockwork speedboat.
Largest of the Lindstrom boats.

Left: (L-1) 1930's 8″ clockwork powered ferry.
Right: (L-13) 8″ nonpowered showboat.
Toy makers always strove to utilize the
parts of one toy for another.

Although not positively identified, these two 11″
clockwork liners have many Lindstrom characteristics.

(LL-1) 17″. In 1934 Lionel introduced their first boat #43 shown here in the foreground. It was quickly followed the next year by #44 (LL-2). By 1937 they were no longer cataloged. Both speedboats are clockwork powered.

Rear: (NY-1) 14″ clockwork *Scout*. Front, left to right: (NY-2) 14″ clockwork *Sportster*, (NY-3) 14″ clockwork *Sea Gull*. All are wooden from the 1950's and have metal trim. The two clockwork outboard motors are reminiscent of those made by Lindstrom.

Two 14″ ships from the 1950's. The Luxury Liner *Caribbean* (MX-1) and The Sparkling Battleship *USS Washington* (MX-2) utilize most of the same metalwork. Marx manufactured few boats in the US; most were imported from Japan.

Left to right:
(MX-8) 7″ liner with detachable battery powered motor,
(MX-5) set of three 7″ warships with a detachable motor,
(MX-6) 6″ speedboat with detachable electric motor.
All these plastic boats were made in the 1960's.

1930's wooden speedboats with
brass trim and clockwork motors.
Rear: (MG-2) 18″ #580 *Miss America.*
Front: (MG-1) 14″ #575 *Miss America.*
Each is made from a solid block of hardwood.

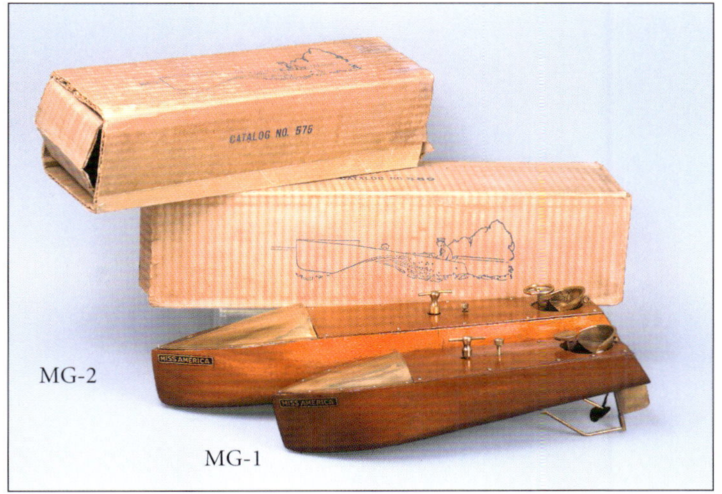

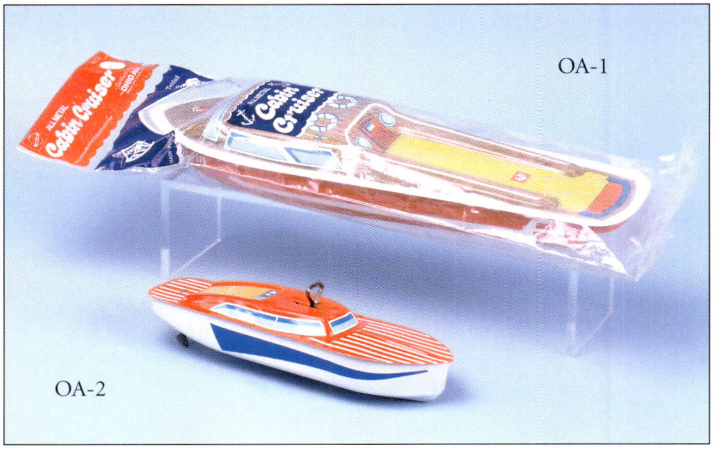

Ohio Art

Front:
(OA-2) 8″ clockwork powered speedboat.
Rear: (OA-1) 14″ nonpowered cabin
cruiser. From their design, both boats
appear to be from the 1960-1980 period.

M&P Mfg. Co. (Roll-O-Float)

(M&P-4) 1950's, 15″ ocean liner *Washington.*
A handsome addition to the wooden,
nonpowered *Roll-O-Float* line of ships.

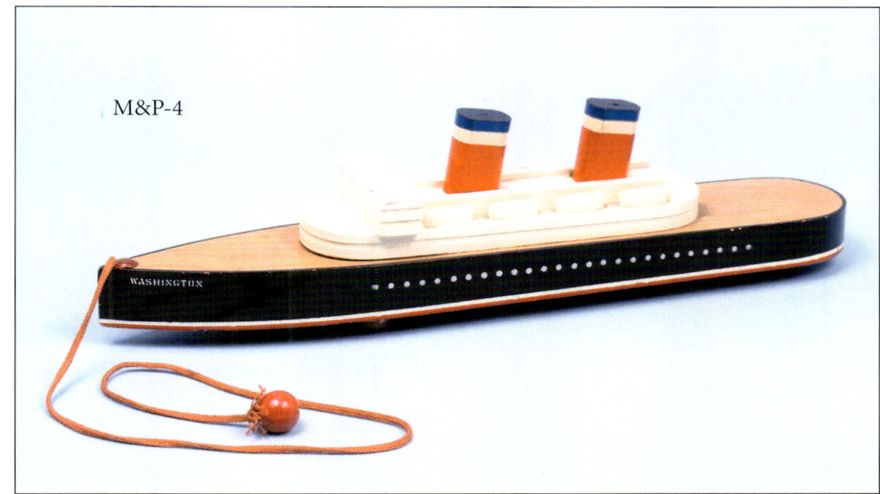

Left to right: (M&P-1) 14″ #311 fireboat,
(M&P-3) 8″ tug, (M&P-2) 14″ freighter.
All are from the 1950's, are wooden,
nonpowered and have ball rollers set
into their hull bottoms.

23

Top: (OR-3) 1920's, 25″ series I super-dreadnaught *USS New York*.
Bottom: (OR-7) 1920's, 25″ series I super-dreadnaught *USS New Mexico*.

Top: (OR-4) 1920's, 35″ series I super-dreadnaught *USS Constitution*.
Bottom: (OR-8) 1920's, 30″ series I super-dreadnaught *USS Pennsylvania*. Interestingly, the *USS Constitution* was laid down in 1920 as a battle cruiser, but was canceled in 1923 due to the Washington Naval Treaty.

24

1920's, series I, Top to bottom:
(OR-13) 22″ super-dreadnaught *USS Nevada,*
(OR-11) 15″ cutter *USS Chaser.*
The *Nevada* was the only battleship at
Pearl Harbor to get underway during the
Japanese attack of Dec. 7, 1941.
During the U.S. Navy's modernization
program of the 1920's and 30's most of
the cage masts were replaced by more
stable tripod masts.

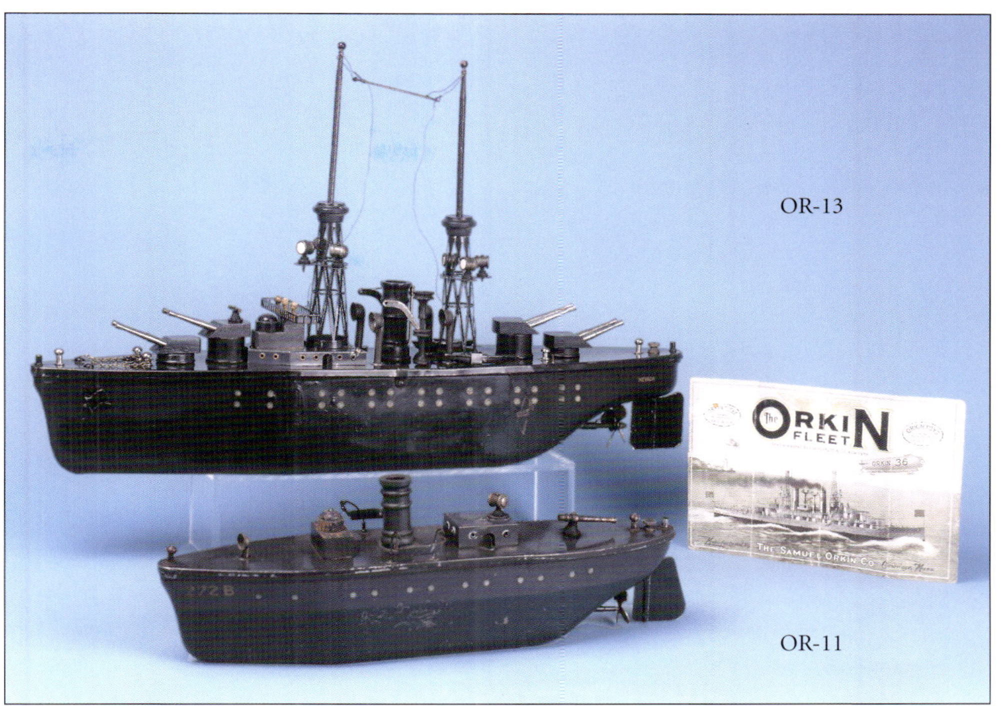

OR-13

OR-11

OR-9

OR-2

1920's. Left to right: (CR-9) 18″ series I destroyer,
(OR-2) 18″ series I cruiser *USS Marcella.*

OR-15

(OR-15) 1920's, 30″ series I super-dreadnaught
USS Texas. Like its real-life namesake, this toy
has three aft turrets.

(OR-14) 1929, 34″ series II, B-1 battleship; (OR-10) 1929, 20″ series II, No. 74 revenue cutter. This series of ships contained two destroyers, two cutters and several variants of the battleship.

(OR-6) 1930's, 23″ speedboat.
Calwis Industries Ltd. of Beverly Hills, CA bought the Orkin name and completely revised the line of boats. In 1932 they offered eight different pleasure boats. Some had steel hulls while others, like the one shown, had what was promoted as "1/8 inch warp-less wood over a sturdy wood frame. Finished in finest weather-proof Egyptian lacquer."

Top: (OR-1) 1920's, Series III, 18″ liner.
Left to right: (OR-12) Series III, 13″ speedboat; (OR-5) series III, 15″ liner. Like all Orkins, these boats are clockwork powered. The ships of this final series are distinguished by their copper hulls. The ship on the right has been repainted, but it originally looked like the others.

(RD-1) 1890, 31″ pull toy paper on wood cruiser *Philadelphia.* Cleverly constructed so that all parts could be stored within its hull, this toy boat fairly represents the outline of the real protected cruiser *Philadelphia* of 1889.

(RN-Group) Found as old store stock with wrapping paper still stuck to their sides, these wooden floor/water toys are typical of those made during the 1930's and 40's for bathtub or beach use. They are marked "Robin Toys."

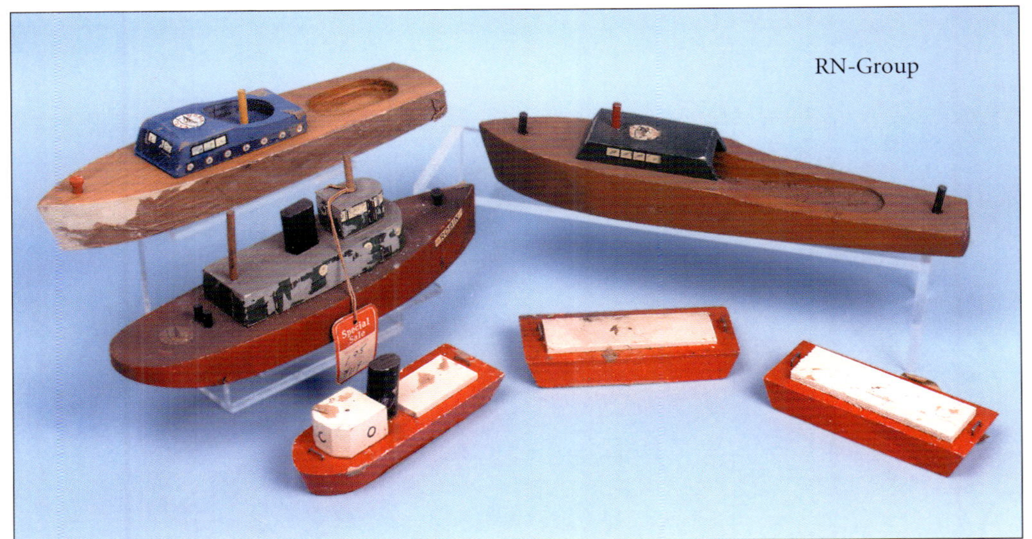

(SE-4) 1907-20, 12″ inertia driven Hill Climber Cruiser #35. The D.P. Clark, Schieble and Dayton names have intertwined, litigious, and confusing histories, making it difficult to vet any "Hill Climber" type of toy. In this case, the box is the answer.

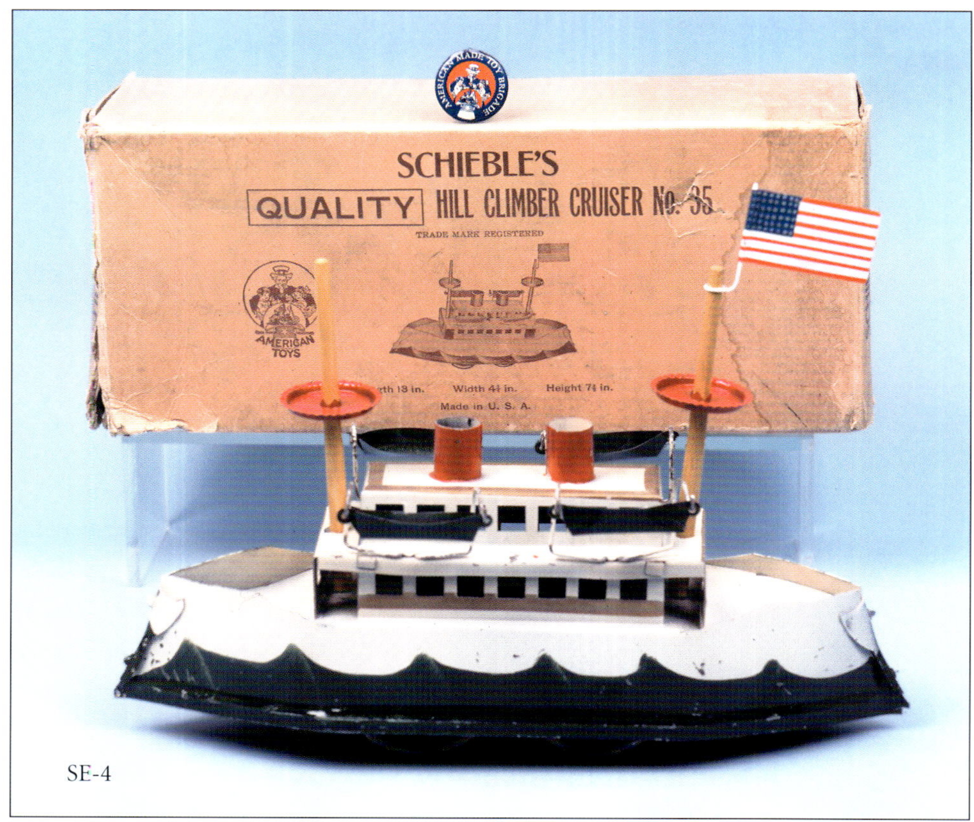

SE-4

SE-2

SE-1

Rear: (SE-2) 15″. Front: (SE-1) 10″.
Both have inertia or "Hill Climber" mechanisms.
They could date anywhere from 1900 to 1930.
These two are shown in the 1921
Butler Brothers Catalog.

Left: (SE-3) **18″**. Right (SE-5) **19″**. Both have virtually the same dimensions and inertia power. The ship on the right is more intricately painted, thus perhaps the older of the two.

(SE-6) **18″**. A "Hill Climber" type motor powers this marble firing battleship.

Patented in 1915, these games became very popular and are still quite often found (in pieces) today. On the left: (SC-3) is set #280/50 with a 12″ battleship and an attacking 6″ submarine. On the right: (SC-4) is set #180/100. It came with two subs and a larger 14″ battleship. The trick was to hit the red target button on the side of the ship with the torpedo, thus releasing the mousetrap mechanism inside. Lesser points were scored by knocking off various parts of the ship.

(SK-1) 1950's, 7″ rubber band driven wooden paddle-wheeler. These novel boats were sold individually in St. Louis as souvenirs as late as the 1990's.

DIRECTIONS   Do Not Put These Boats In Water

THEY ARE INTENDED TO BE PLAYED WITH ON THE TABLE OR FLOOR

To prepare the Dreadnought for action first remove the deck. In the hull you will find a spring similar to a mouse-trap. Hold the boat tight with the left hand and with the right hand raise the spring and turn it over until it catches hold of the little notch in the trigger.

Keep your fingers away from the red target on the side of the Dreadnought, as the least touch of the target will cause the trigger to release the spring. After you have the spring set, replace the deck, turrets, smoke-stacks, etc.

The Submarine is arranged inwardly with a spring with which to shoot the wooden torpedo. To load the Submarine, simply insert the torpedo into the hole in front of the boat and push back until the trigger catches and holds it.

Place the boats on the table or floor about two or three feet apart. Place the Dreadnought so that the red target will face the Submarine. Take a good aim and press down on the trigger of the Submarine, which will immediately discharge the torpedo. If your aim is good and you hit the red target you will behold a most realistic view of blowing up a battle-ship.

A1250 415

During WW II Strombeck-Becker produced a number of solid wood scale model kits whose simple construction made them more toys than display models. Clockwise from the center rear: (STR-1) 12″ cruiser *U.S.S. Indianapolis,* (STR-3) 12″ aircraft carrier *U.S.S. Yorktown,* (STR-2) 10″ battleship *U.S.S. California,* (STR-5) 11″ submarine *U.S.S. Nautilus,* (STR-4) 11 3/8″ destroyer *U.S.S. Warrington.*

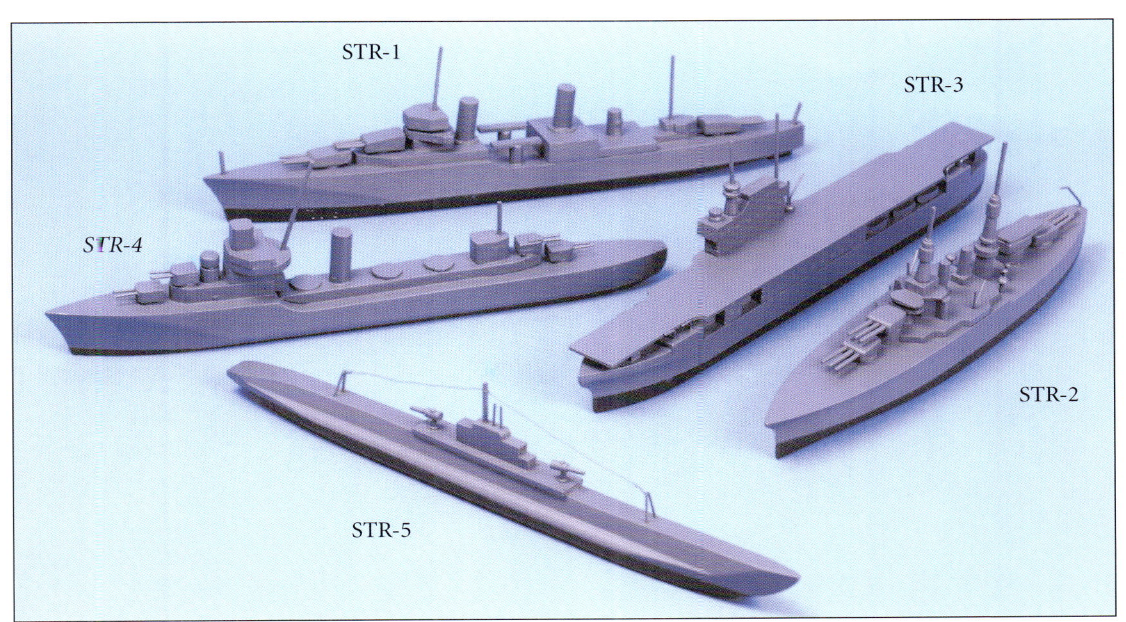

1920's. Front, left to right: (SS-2) 9″ #28 speedboat, (SS-4) 9″ *Sail-A-Way,* (SS-1) 9″ #28 speedboat. Rear: (SS-3) 9″ #38 *Miami Sea Sled.* All are spring driven. Ferdinand Strauss is reputed to be the founder of mass-produced mechanical toys in the U.S.

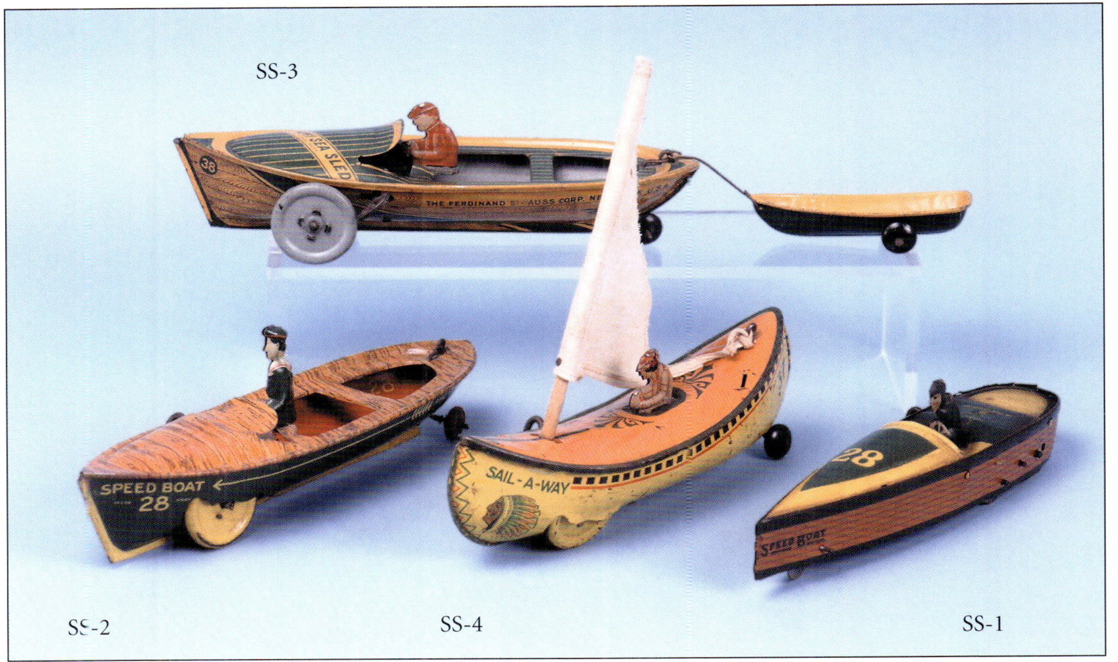

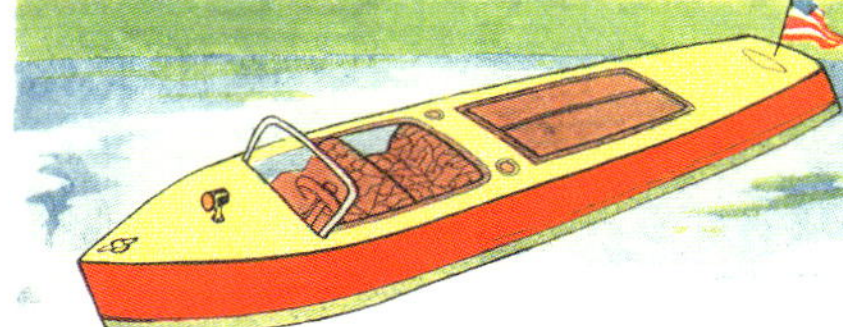

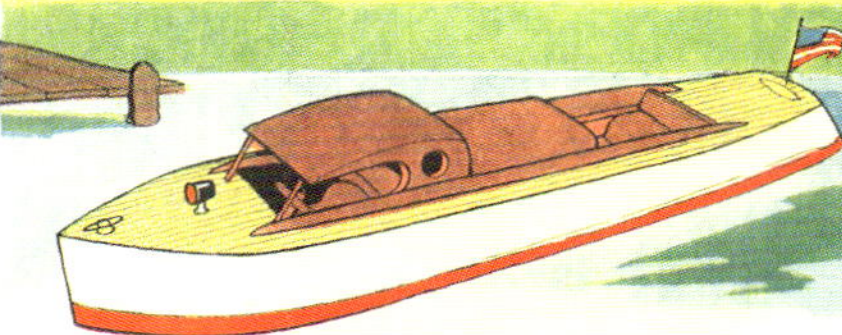

(TM-14) 1930's, 16″ freighter *Mohawk*. The 1930 *Supplee-Biddle* hardware catalog (Philadelphia, PA) listed the freighter plus a fireboat and a speedboat. Each was priced at 67 cents!

TM-14

TM-2   TM-1

Left: (TM-2) 1930, 19″ destroyer.
Right: (TM-1) 1930, 15″ battleship *Washington*.
These ships were produced by the original Tillicum Co. of Tacoma, WA.

Left: (TM-4) 1930's, 11″ liner.
Right: (TM-3) 1930's, Battle Fleet No.115.
Both sets are from Tillicum
Sales Corp., NYC.

During the 1940's and WW II,
Tillicum toys reflected the national purpose.
Left: (TM-5) Convoy Set No.T-104.
Right: (TM-7) National Defense Set No.T-106.

(TM-11) late 1930's, Coast Defense Set No. T-303.
Milton Bradley took over Tillicum c.1938
and began expanding the line with sets.

Two late version (1950's) sets.
Left: (TM-15) **Harbor Sport Set.**
Right: (TM-16) **Coastwise Set No. T-610.**
Both sets have plastic tops on the ships.

Left to right:
(TM-10) **Jr. Harbor Set No. T-205,** (TM-6) **Harbor Set No. T-105,**
(TM-8) **Tiny Set No. T-80,** (TM-9) **Junior Yacht Set No. T-202.**
All these sets were made in the late 1930's and into the 1940's.

Rear: (TM-12)
carried by FAO Schwarz in 1952,
Ocean Travel Set No. T-600.
Front: (TM-13)
early 1950's, Harbor Master Set No. T-630.
After WW II, as plastic came into
use, Tillicum ships took on
plastic tops as seen here.

(TG-1) 1940.
One of many wooden boat block construction sets available for the budding naval architect during the 20th century.

TG-1

Little is known about the manufacturer of these wooden boat sets. They seem to be from the 1940-50 era.
Front to rear: (TBN-1) Set #2, 2 boats and 3 barges;
(TBN-2) Set #4, 6 boats and 2 barges;
(TBN-3) Set #5, 7 boats and 4 barges.

TBN-3
TBN-1
TBN-2

The Dowst Mfg. Co. exploded into ships in 1939. The sets shown contain most of their different types of die-cast floor toy ships offered during WW II.
Clockwise from left:
(TT-1) Naval Defense Set, 13 ships;
(TT-2) #5900 Convoy Set, 13 ships;
(TT-4) #5750 Navy Set, 6 ships;
(TT-7) Sea Champions, 5 ships;
(TT-3) #5700, Fleet Set, 12 ships.

TT-1
TT-2
TT-4
TT-3
TT-7

35

(UK-64) 24″. This well-made steam powered speedboat is a mystery. Its design seems to date it to 1900-1910. The hull and superstructure are fashioned from light gauge tinplate, while the boiler and stack are brass. I believe it is US in origin, however, a case could be made otherwise.

UK-64

Union Mfg. Co.

UN-1

Several sizes of these steam powered boats often attributed to Buckman were manufactured between 1853 and 1869 when the company was acquired by Hull & Stafford. Left to right: (UN-3) 12″ #50, (UN-2) 9″ #76, (UN-1) 18″ #55.

Walbert Mfg. Co.

Left: (WT-2) 1921-27, 13″ ferry. This clockwork floor toy was shown in the Wolverine catalog after their takeover in 1927.
Right: (WT-1) 1915, 14″ battleship. The nonpowered ship has two compartments connected by a hinge. They separate and fill with water when the target latch is released after being struck by a torpedo.

(WD-4) 1879-1904, 12″ steamboat *Water Witch*. Typical of Weeden's steam powered boats, of which there were 8 models in the years 1879-1933, *Water Witch* had a built-in tank / wick system which simplified the firing of her boiler.

Left to right:
(WD-1) 1899-1918, 15″ torpedo bow boat #1, *Dewey;*
(WD-3) 1898-1933, 15″ standard bow boat #1;
(WD-2) 1899-1918, 15″ variant of torpedo bow boat #1.
Hull sizes ranged from 12″ to the largest of 20″ which had two stacks.

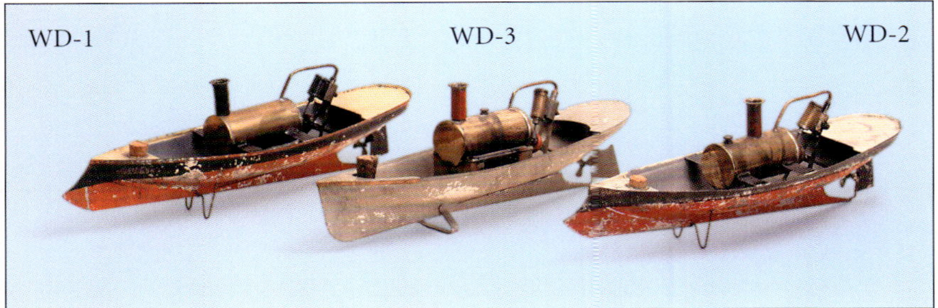

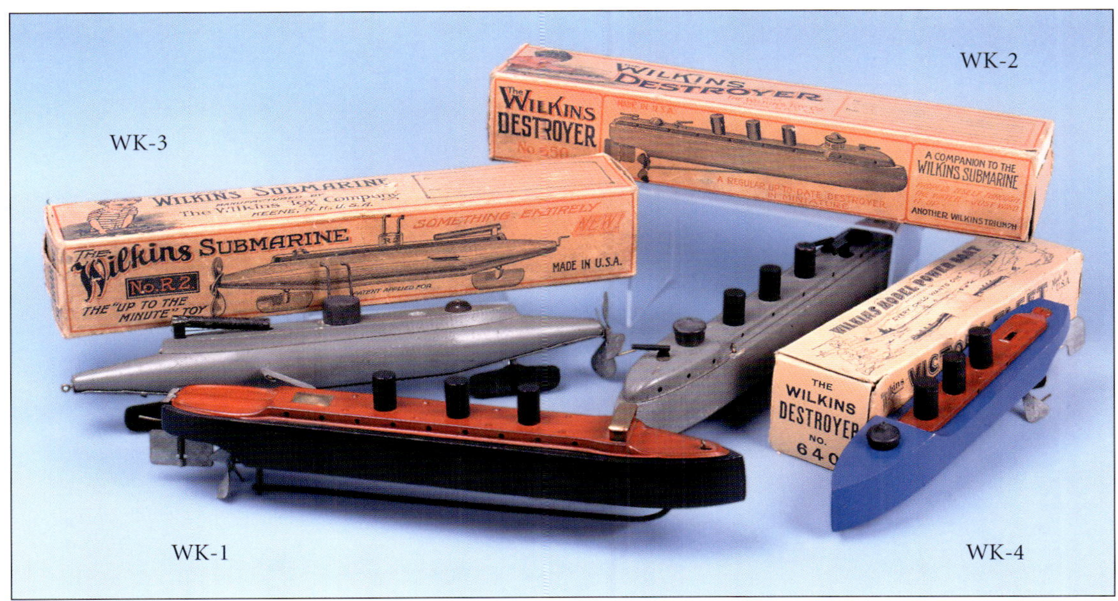

1919-1921. Rear, left to right:
(WK-3) (introduced 1917)
14″ No. R 2 submarine,
(WK-2) 14″ No. 650 destroyer.
Front, left to right:
(WK-1) 14″ No. 655 transport,
(WK-4) 11″ No. 640 destroyer.
Altogether there are five wooden rubber band powered ships in this series including an 11″ transport.

Clockwise from top left: (W-1), (W-10), (W-12) and (W-2).
Late 1940's, 14″ Variations of #93 Luxury Liner. The two on the right are earlier versions which utilize the same sheet metal as the battleship.

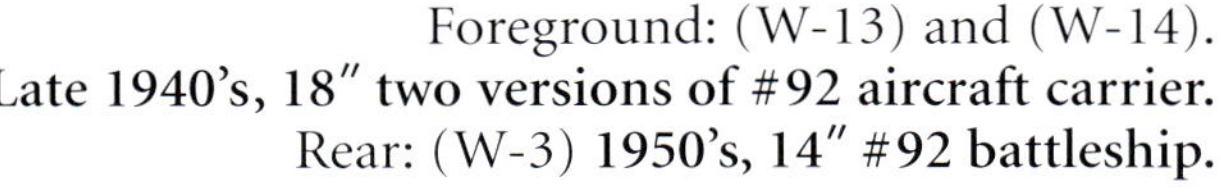

Foreground: (W-13) and (W-14).
**Late 1940's, 18″ two versions of #92 aircraft carrier.
Rear: (W-3) 1950's, 14″ #92 battleship.**

(W-16) 1950's, 16″ barge.
Uses the hull of the aircraft carrier.

Left to right: (WE-3) **1941, 12″ #406 aircraft carrier;** (WE-1) **1940-46, 12″ #404 ocean liner** *S.S. America;* (WE-4) **1941, 7″ #227 ocean liner. All are nonpowered and are meant for use on land or sea. The** *China Clipper* **overhead was manufactured in various versions from 1935 to 1946.**

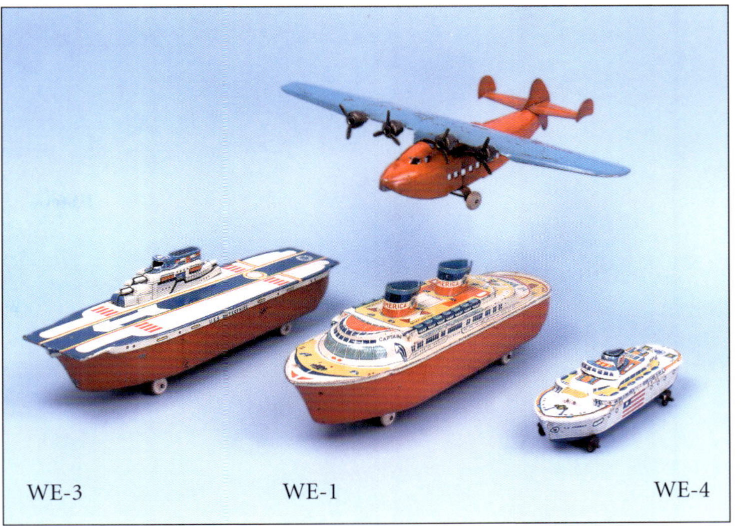

WE-3   WE-1   WE-4

Left to right: (W-11), (W-15) and (W-5).
Late 1940's and 50's, 13″ variants of #87 submarine.

W-11   W-15   W-5

W-6

W-4

W-7   W-9   W-8

Left to right: (W-6), (W-7), (W-4), (W-9) and (W-8).
1950's, 13″ later versions of #87 submarine.
The two on the right are the final incarnation.

WE-2

(WE-2) **A great example of a 1930's beach toy.**

39

British Manufacturers

Made during the 1930's, these steam powered speedboats were made in many sizes. Due to their wooden hulls, however, their life-span was limited. Rear to front: (BN-2) 26″ *Seahawk*, (BN-3) 21″ *Swallow*, (BN-1) 19″ *Swallow*.

Bowman Models, Ltd.

More elaborate than most (BN-5) 26″ *Seahawk* is a trim steam driven cabin cruiser. *Aeroboat II* (BN-4) 30″ is an odd departure in propulsion since it is powered by rubber bands. Both have the typical Bowman wooden hull.

NAME	LOCATION	DATES	FOUNDER	PAGE
Bell	–	–	–	41
Bowman Models Ltd.	Dereham, Norfolk	1923-34 & 1946-48	–	40
Cowan De Groot, Ltd. (Codeg)	–	1919 to date	S. Cowan & A. De Groot	41
Flory	Bromley, Kent	–	Harold Flory	41
Hornby/Meccano	Liverpool	1901 to date	Frank Hornby	42-43
London Stereoscopic & Photo.Co.	London	–	–	44
Mills Bros., Ltd. (Milbro)	Scotland	1919-1930's	–	44
Star	Birkenhead, Merseyside	–	–	44
Sutcliffe Pressings Ltd.	Horsforth, Leeds	1885-1982	J. William Sutcliffe	45-47
Triang /Lines Bros.	Merton, London	1919-1971	Walter Lines	48
Unknown	various	–	–	49
Wells - Brimtoy	Hollyhead, Wales	1919-1965	A. Wells	49

Right: (BE-1) 4″ is a British-made plastic puzzle. Left: (BE-1A) is an identical Japanese version in wood. Who copied from whom?

BE-1A

BE-1

Cowan De Groot, Ltd. (Codeg)

(CG-1) 1950's, 11″ sturdily made *put-put* launch.

CG-1

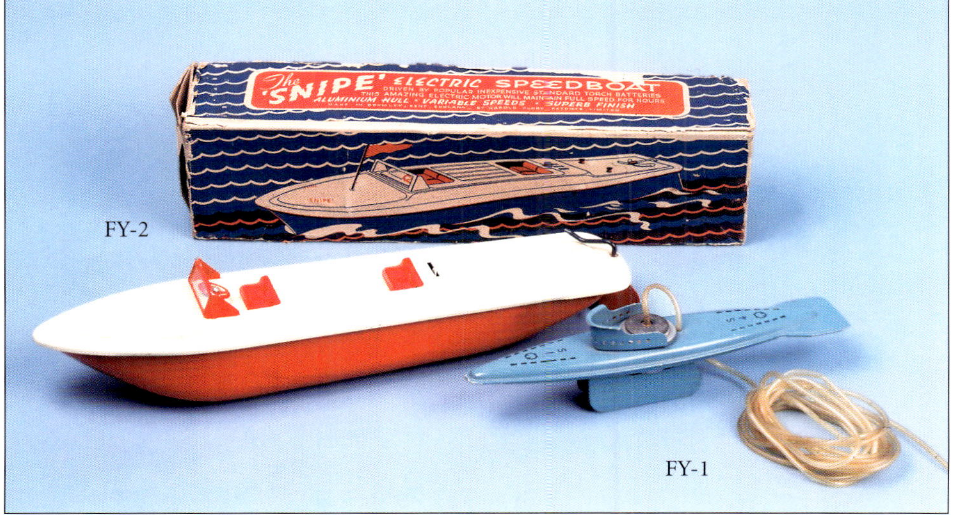

FY-2

FY-1

Flory

Left to right: (FY-2) 14″ battery powered speedboat *Snipe*, (FY-1) 9″ submarine *S4*. The sub dives or rises by pumping air through the tube.

During the 1930's Hornby boats were also produced in France.
Top to bottom:
(ME-3) 12″ speedboat No. 2 *Pegase*,
(ME-10) 9″ speedboat No. 1.

1933-1939 Left: (ME-11) 16″ cabin cruiser No. 5 *Viking*.
Right: (ME-13) 16″ limousine boat No. 4 *Venture*.
Both of these clockwork boats came painted in red and cream, blue and white, and green and ivory color schemes.

ME-3

ME-10

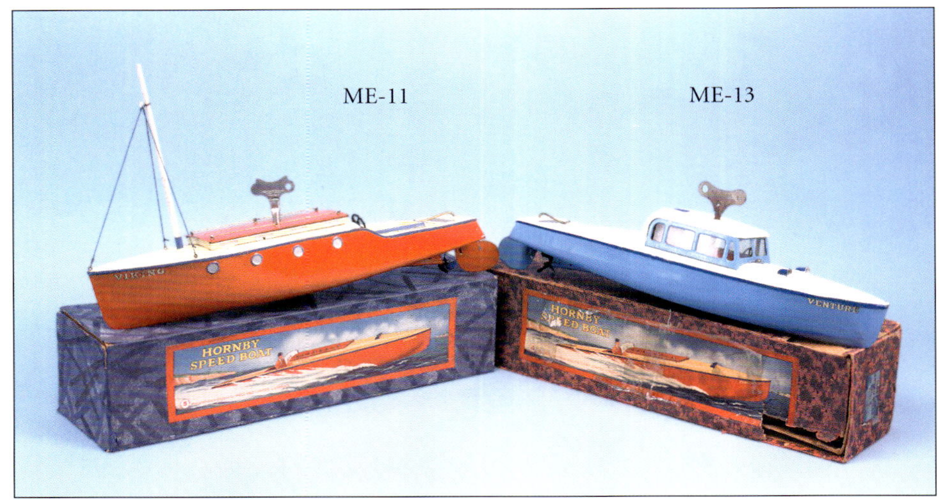

ME-11

ME-13

ME-1

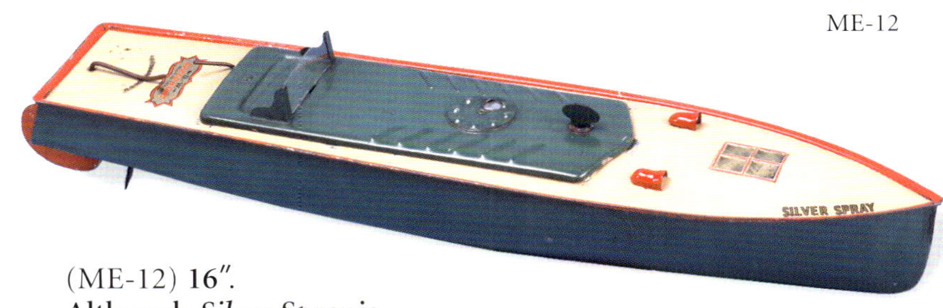

ME-12

(ME-1)
1934-39, 6″ Dinky Toy No. 534 *Queen Mary*. This ship launched an extensive series of water-line 1-150 scale toys that could be a collecting category unto itself. Pre-WW II there were several sets and at least 8 different liners and 10 warships.

(ME-12) 16″.
Although *Silver Spray* is trademarked *D-W*, it has all the characteristics of Hornby, including its clockwork mechanism.

Between 1933 and 1939, Hornby made three clockwork boats called *speedboats* and three called *racing boats.*
Back: (ME-6) 16″ racing boat No. 3 *Racer III.*
Middle, left to right: (ME-5) 16″ speedboat No. 3 *Curlew,* (ME-4) 12″ speedboat No. 2 *Swift.*
Front, left to right: (ME-7) 9″ speedboat No. 1 *Hawk,* (ME-2) 8″ racing boat No. 1 *Racer I.*

ME-6

ME-5

ME-4

ME-7

ME-2

(SPC-1) Late 19th century, 5″ *Swift.*
The boat has a double bottom to store fuel,
which when burned creates hot air to expel
through a tube for propulsion.

(SY-3) 1980's, 21″
Pacific Star. Made
in several sizes,
Star yachts have
wooden hulls and
cotton sails.

(MO-1) 1930's, 28″ *Alisa Yacht* has a wooden hull
and deck. The sail is well fashioned from nylon.

Group of clockwork boats from 1960's & 1970's.
Rear, left to right:
(S-11) 9″ *Jupiter*,
(S-17) 12″ *Diana*,
special collectors' edition.
Front, left to right:
(S-8) 9″ *Sprite*,
(S-12) 12″ *Commodore*.

Rear: (S-7) 1930's, 20″ clockwork speedboat was one of Sutcliffe's largest offerings.
Front: (S-21) 1930's, 12″ clockwork speedboat.

Clockwork speedboats of the 1960's & 1970's:
Rear: (S-15) 9″ *Tiger*.
Middle row, left to right: (S-18) 12″ *Merlin*, (S-9) 12″ *Hawk*.
Front: (S-13) 9″ *Racer 1*.

Manufactured for years (1930's-1970's), this 7″ clockwork submarine came in many variants. The oldest (S-3) is seen in the foreground. Middle row, left to right: (S-4), (S-5). Top: (S-6).

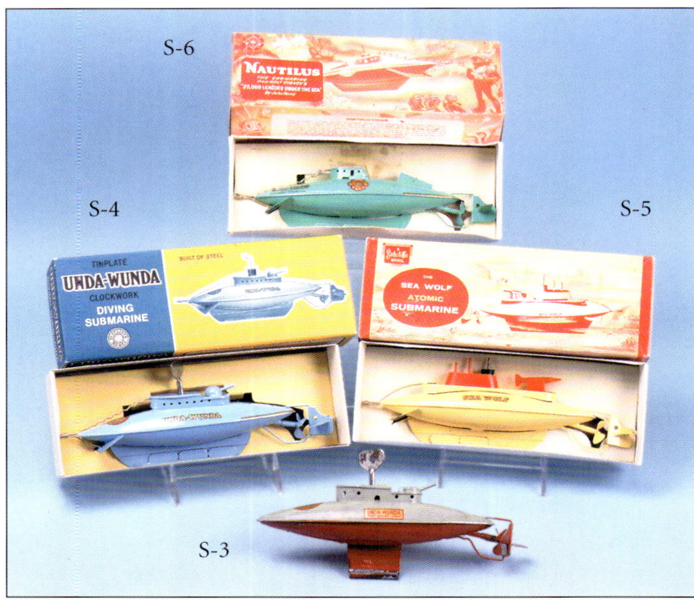

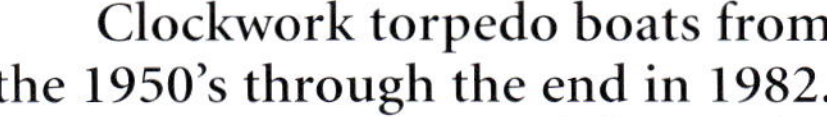

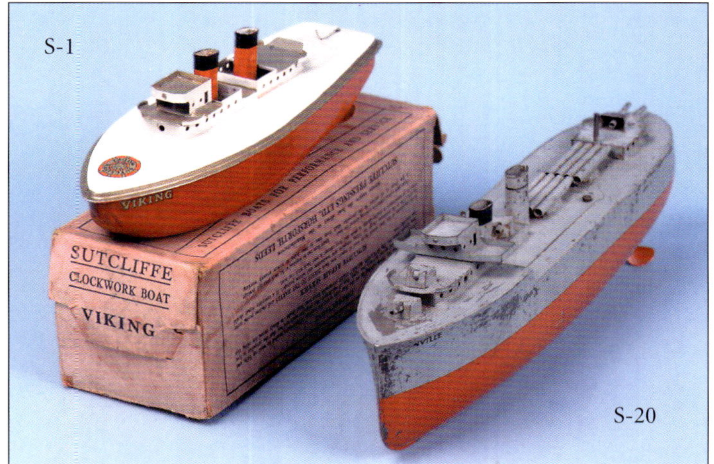

Clockwork torpedo boats from the 1950's through the end in 1982.
Rear, left to right:
(S-24) 9″ *Fury*,
(S-16) 9″ *Victor*.
Front: (S-22) 9″.

Left: (S-1) 1950, 9″ liner *Viking*.
Right: (S-20) 1938-40, 12″ destroyer *Grenville*.

S-19

S-23

Two boats reminiscent of Sir Malcolm Campbell's *Bluebird* speedboat series.
Left to right:
(S-23) 12″ *Bluebird II*,
(S-19) 10″ *Bluebird*.
In the late 1930's, using an engine from one of his record breaking racing cars, Campbell proceeded to take the world water speed records.

S-2

S-10

S-14

Rear: (S-2) 1978-80, 12″ clockwork battleship *Valiant*.
Front, left to right:
(S-10) 1920-28, 12″ "put-put" engine battleship;
(S-14) 1930's clockwork battleship.

Rear: (TR-4) 12″ #110 speedboat.
Front: (TR-1) 9″ speedboat. Both are clockwork.

**Steel-hulled sailboats came in several
sizes during the 1930's and 1950's.**
Rear: (TR-6) 21″.
Middle, left to right: (TR-5) 16″,
(TR-3) 14″, (TR-2) 10″.
Front: (TR-1) 9″ speedboat.

(CF-1) 1928, 15″ Biscuit tin and floor toy *Berengaria*. The actual manufacturer of the Crawford's tin is unknown. Launched in 1912 as the HAPAG *Imperator*, the real ship, after seizure and use as a troop transport, was ceded to Britain and at first leased, then sold to Cunard who renamed her *Berengaria*.

CF-1

(UK-67) 8″ This post-WW II British-made speedboat is powered by a flywheel motor. It has many of the features of contemporary Japanese offerings.

UK-67

Top: (CK-7) Kellerman, 1928, 9″ #287 paddle-wheeler. Bottom: (WB-1) Wells-Brimtoy, 1951, 9″ #70 paddle-wheeler. Both boats are clockwork and operate on the floor or in the water.

CK-7

WB-1

Czechoslovakian Manufacturer

Rear: (HH-1) 10″ clockwork liner.
Front: (HH-2) 7″ clockwork liner, marked "made in Czechoslovakia" on the bottom. Little is known about this manufacturer. The ships appear to be of a 1930's vintage.

French Manufacturers

Bonnet & Cie—Vebe

These two 8″ clockwork boats were made in the 1930's. Left to right: (BV-2) #25 sparkling (from the aft stack) liner. The liner also came in a three stack version (see page 53). (BV-1) #24 sparkling cannon boat.

NAME	LOCATION	DATES	FOUNDER	PAGE
Bonnet & CIE - VEBE	Paris	1921-1960	Victor Bonnet	51
GIL (Jouet Gil)	Paris	1947-1978	Gilbert Dutrou	52
Gutmann (Memo)	Paris	–	Mery Gutmann	53
JEP, JDP, et al	Paris	1902-1968	Roussel & Dufrien	54-55
JRD	Paris	1938-1961	Jean Donot	56
JIF, Jouet Francais	Paris	–	–	56
Jouets Charlys	St.- Rambert - D'Albon	–	–	56
Lefevre, E. F.	Paris	1860-1897	Edmund Faivre	57-58
Mignot-C.B.G.	Paris	1825 to date	Henri Mignot	59
Nova	Paris	1918-1968	M. Fradet	59
Radiguet (& Massiot)	Paris	1872-1905	–	60-61
Rossignol-C.R.	Paris	1868-1962	Charles Rossignol	62
Unknown	–	–	–	63

Two torpedo boats from the
late 1960's and early 1970's.
Left: (GL-4) 25″ U 52.
Right (GL-1) 19″ U 25.
Both have battery powered
electric motors.

(GL-3) 1960-70, 20″ electric powered cabin cruiser.
Gil boats were built with heavy sheet metal,
thus extremely sturdy.

(GL-2) 1970's, 26″ battery powered S63 submarine.
A very well-made boat, rotation of its periscopes
controlled diving and power.

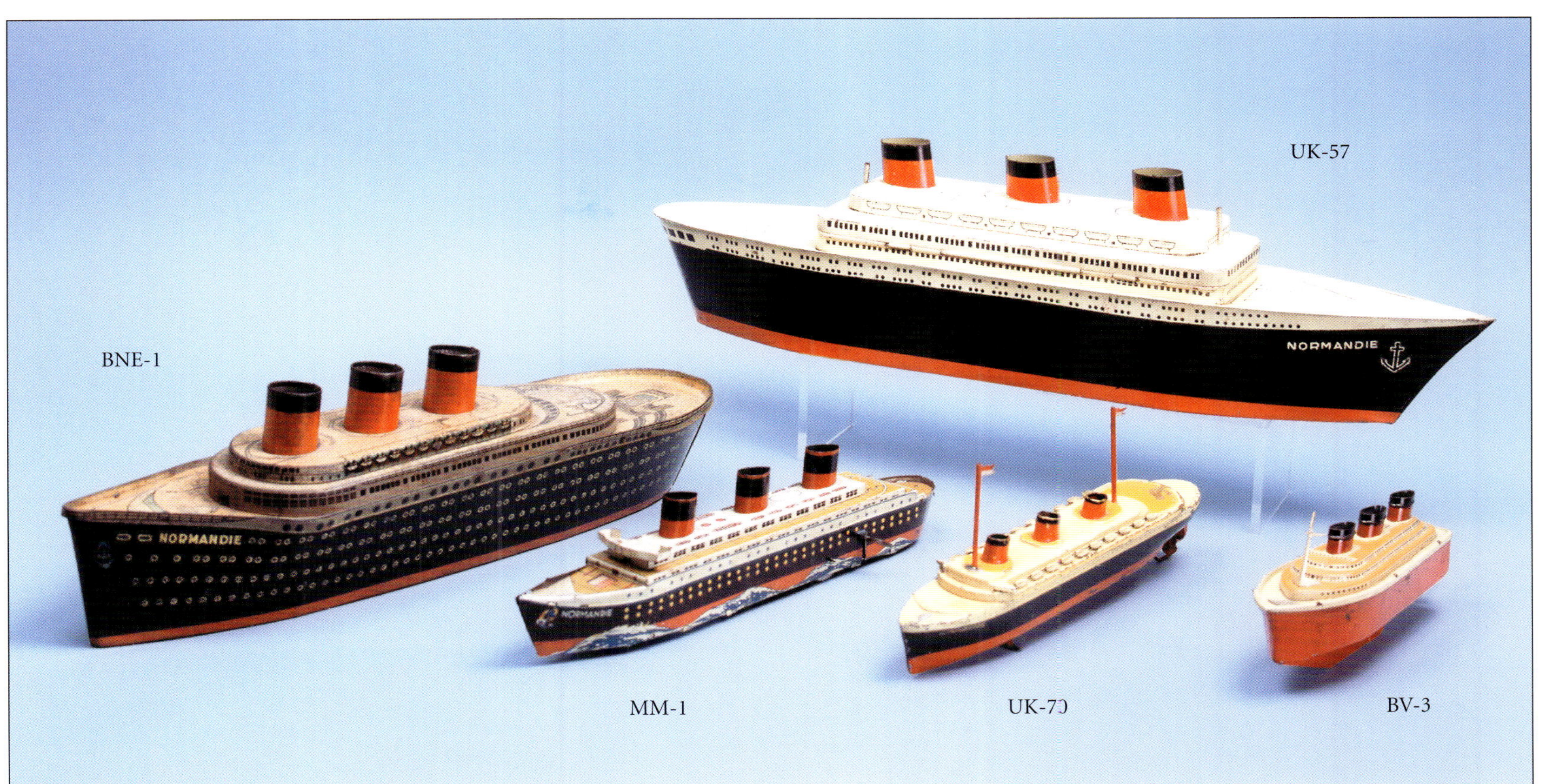

Gutmann (Memo)

The *Normandie* was the pride of The French Line (CGT) and arguably the most beautiful liner to ever sail the seas. On her maiden voyage, May 5, 1935, she captured the Blue Riband with an average speed of 29.98 knots between Bishops Rock and Ambrose Light, a feat she would exceed on the return voyage. The pride in this great engineering achievement is displayed by the toys of the times.
Rear: (UK-57) 22″ Galettes St. Michel biscuit tin of an unknown maker.
Front left to right: (BNE-1) 18″ biscuit tin marked "Geslot Voreux" on the aft deck and "H. Bethune A Bouchain (Nord)" at the aft port waterline, (MM-1) 13″ Memo #814, (UK-70) 11″ manufacturer unknown, (BV-3) VEBE 8″. This version has three stacks and the name *Normandie* embossed at the bow.

Clockwise from left rear:
(J-12) **1932-39, 13″ #912-6** ocean liner *Normandie;*
(J-2) **1938-66, 14″ #916.3** ocean liner;
(J-15) **1932-41, 8″ #912.1** ocean liner.

54

Rear: (J-3) **1918-24, 19″ #915.1** torpedo boat.
One of the failings of directly comparing toys
with their real life counterparts is the time element.
In this case the boat imitates an obsolete design,
20 years old at its time of manufacture.
Front: (J-13) **1920-29, 11″ #913.2** cruiser.

Available from the 1930's to 1960, these sturdy
clockwork speedboats came in five sizes and three colors.
Rear to front: (J-11) 16″ #913-4 *JEP 4*, (J-16) 14″ #913-3 *JEP 3*,
(J-17) 10″ #913-2 *JEP 2*, (J-19) 10″ #912.2 *Typhon*.

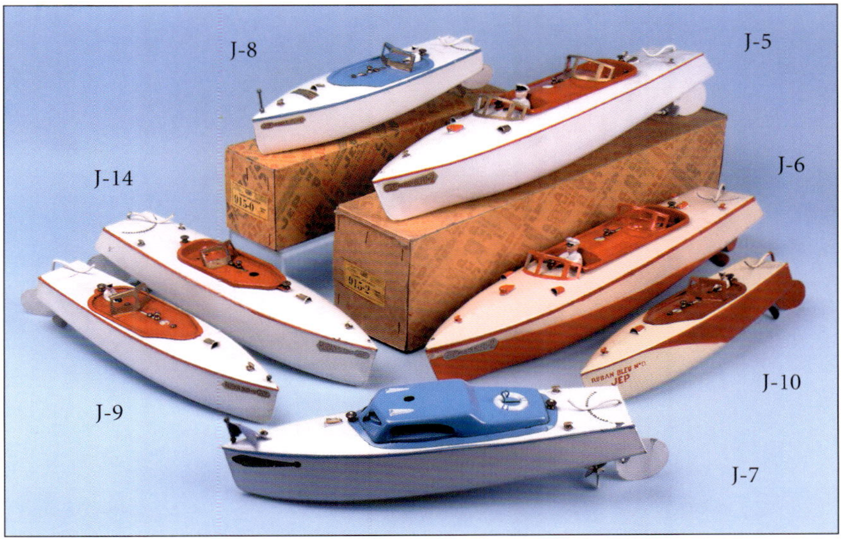

The Blue Ribbon series of clockwork speedboats was
produced from 1938 to 1966. Pre-WW II versions
have an angularly striped hull paint scheme.
Clockwise from the left:
(J-9) 12″ #915.0 *Ruban Bleu No. 0*,
(J-14) 13″ #915.1 *Ruban Bleu No. 1*,
(J-8) 12″ #915.0 *Ruban Bleu No. 0*,
(J-5) 19″ #915.2 *Ruban Bleu No 2*,
(J-6) 19″ #915.2 *Ruban Bleu No. 2*,
(J-10) 12″ #915.0 *Ruban Blue No. 0*,
(J-7) 13″ #915.1 cabin cruiser *Ruban Bleu No. 1*.

Left to right:
(J-4) 1951-66, 15″ #919 submarine *Nautilus*;
(J-1) 1936-50, 15″ #918 submarine *Corsaire*;
(J-18) 1967, 15″ final version of *Nautilus*
with plastic superstructure.

Both submarines from the WW I era (UK-66) 8″ *Foch* and (UK-12) 12″ *Clemenceau* are nonpowered. The boats were also made for export to the U.S. with appropriate flags and American names. They dive or surface by squeezing a rubber ball attached by a tube to a bladder inside of the sub. A wooden extension of the hatch closes it when the vessel dives. Le Berrob won a gold medal at the toy fair in 1916. Its manufacturer, JIF (or IJF), is another enigma.

UK-66

UK-12

56

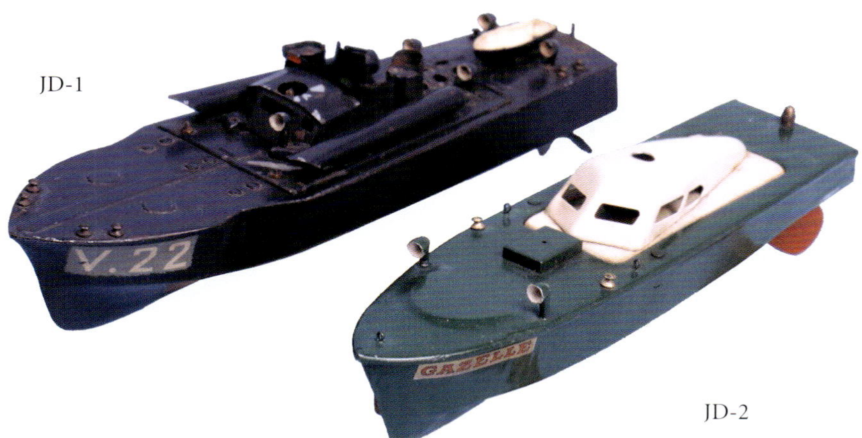

JD-1

JD-2

 Two boats from 1950.
Left to right:
(JD-1) 13″ #5025 torpedo boat *V.22*,
(JD-2) 13″ #5002 cabin cruiser *Gazelle*.
Both are clockwork.

IC-1

 (JC-1) 10″ Battleship *Richelieu*. This is one of the most bizarre toy ships. It depends upon its interior filling of cork for flotation. Little is known about the company that made this toy, and the production date is unknown.

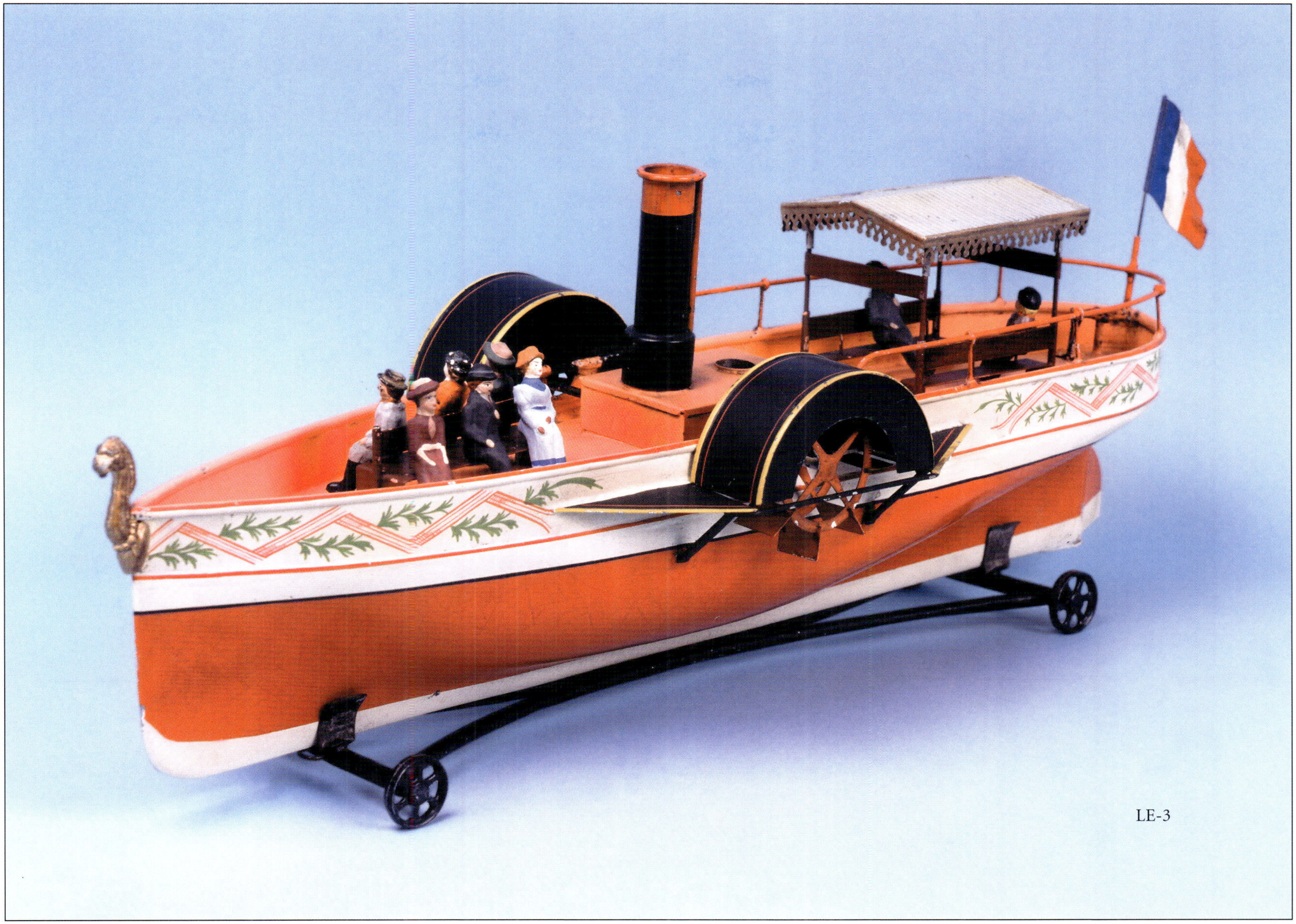

LE-3

(LE-3) 1890's, 21″ clockwork No. 2 paddle-wheeler.
An 1890's E.F. Lefevre catalog claims that it is the successor
to the firms of Dessein, Faivre and G. Potier. The Parisian
company won medals at various expositions from 1867
to 1889. The figurehead and hand-painted filigree work
are typical of their products.

(LE-1) **1890's, 9″ paddle-wheeler No. 2/0. The helmsman is original and is held in place by a pin inserted through a hole in the deck.**

Utilizing the same 18″ hull, these two 1890's clockwork boats are left to right: (LE-4) Cannon boat No. 0 and (LE-2) paddle-wheeler No. 0. From 1902 to 1909 JEP, having incorporated the FV trademark, sold a boat as #973 that was almost identical to the gunboat.

(LE-5) 1890's, 18″ is another version of No. 0 paddle-wheeler. This boat has been professionally restored.

(MFP-1) **1930's, 19″ clockwork wooden speedboat.**
This Parisian company made a whole series of wooden
speedboats and sailboats during its 50 years in business.

MFP-1

MT-2

(MT-2) Although depicting a 1905 engagement
between Japanese and Russian ships, this set is a reissue.
Mignot famously saved all their molds, thus
confounding accurate production dates.

(MT-1) **1905.** This diorama shows various French
warships engaging German and British torpedo
boats. The ship in the upper left is quite similar to
the 1902 armored cruiser *Kleber,* while the
battleship in the lower right is much like the 1903
Patrie. By this time the French had lost their
technical naval superiority of the 1880's to the English.

MT-1

(R-5) 1890, 39″ steam driven battleship. During the 1880's the French were technically advanced over the world's naval powers in armor, artillery and propulsion; however, they retained the outdated tactic of the ram. The elongated bow is typical and an accurate representation of the then current warship designs. The ship has an *Au Nain Bleu* plate on the aft deck, using a Parisian address that predates 1910.

R-5

R-7

(R-7) 1890, 16″ gunboat. This ship has an exceptionally long ram bow. Most Radiguet boats required the removal of the boiler in order to fire up the alcohol burner. The fitting immediately behind the steam dome on the steam line facilitated this procedure.

1890 Rear: (R-4) **22″ cruiser.**
Front, left to right: (R-1) **16″ gunboat,**
(R-3) **15″ launch.** While most
Radiguet boats have wooden decks,
the launch's is copper-painted brass.

(R-6) **11″ pinnace.**
This is unusually small
for a Radiguet.

(R-2) **1890, 26″ cruiser.**
When using ramming tactics, it
was an important design feature
for a ship to be able to fire forward.
This explains the use of blisters to
enable the side guns to extend their
radius of action. This ship has
typically French armored topmasts.
Many fittings and details, such as
guns, railings, boilers and masts
were interchangeable among
Radiguet ships. The copper and
black paint scheme on the zinc
hull is, of course, their most
distinctive feature.

The graphics of the box confirms that these three
flywheel driven floor toys are from the 1900-1910 period.
Rear: (RL-2) 9″ gunboat.
Front, left to right: (RL-1) 6″ gunboat, (RL-4) 4¹/2″ gunboat.
All have an action similar to those boats made by Hess.
They also rock as if upon the waves.

(RL-3) 1950-60, 12″ speedboat.
This boat ends almost 100 years of toy making.

(UK-78) **1900, 7″ submarine.** This rubber band powered vessel for "pond or bathtub" is quite crudely made. Its manufacturer, L.S., is a mystery.

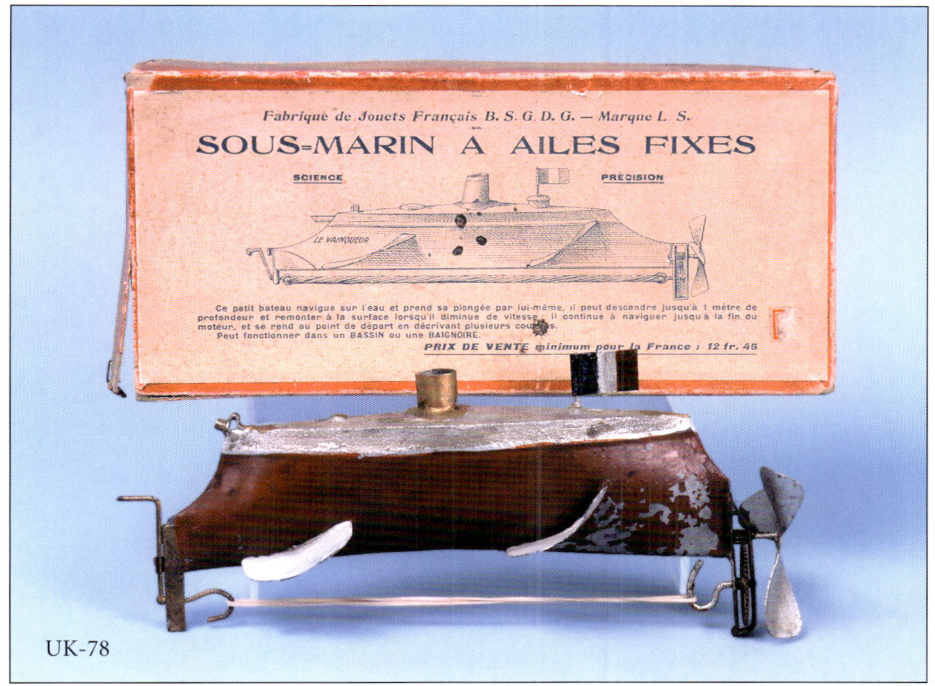

Right: (UK-44) *Le Racer* is similar, yet better made than the U.S. built Gobar put-put boat of the 1930's. Left: (UK-65) 6″ *Le Raceret* is a diminutive cousin.

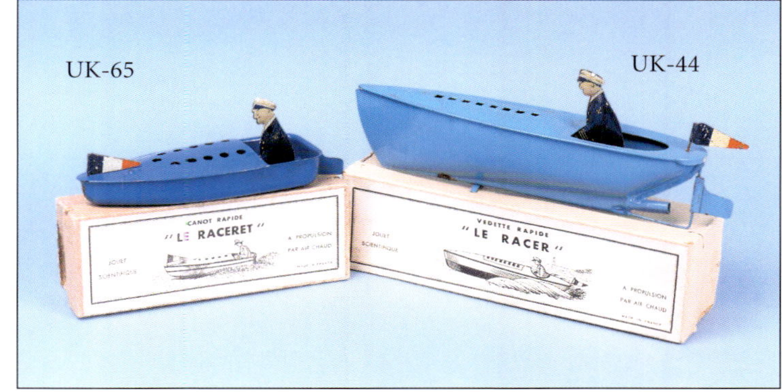

Back: (UK-14) **14″.** Front (UK-90) **15″.** Neither submarine has any identification on its original box, yet both are similar in design and construction to those made by L.S. (see above).

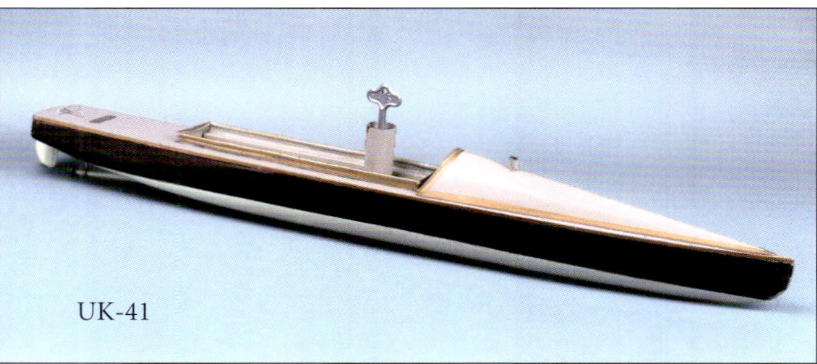

(UK-41) **35″.** This wooden hulled clockwork speedboat has a tag on the aft deck from the famous Parisian toy store *"Au Nain Bleu."* The curved foredeck, stack, and cockpit are sheet metal. While this is obviously a manufactured piece, the only clue as to its manufacturer are the letters "A.S." that appear on the possibly original aluminum key.

German Manufacturers

Arnold, Co.

(A-72) **1950's, 20″ prototype from Arnold's archives.**

NAME	LOCATION	DATES	FOUNDER	PAGE
Arnold, Co.	Nuremberg	1906-1999	Karl Arnold	64-74
Bing, Gebrüder	Nuremberg	1866-1933	Ignatz & A. Bing	75-97
Brandt	–	–	–	98
Büchner	–	–	–	98
Carette, George, et Cie.	Nuremberg	1886-1917	George Carette	99-105, 110, 113
Distler, Johann & Co.	Nuremberg	1900-1962	Johann Distler	106
Einfalt, Gebrüder (Kosmos)	Nuremberg	1922 to date	G. & J. Einfalt	106
Falk, J	Nuremberg	1890-1940	Joseph Falk	107-108, 124
Fischer, Georg	Nuremberg	1899-1932	Georg Fischer	108
Fleischmann, Gebrüder	Nuremberg	1887 to date	Johann Fleischmann	99, 101, 102, 103, 105,109-124
Gescha (Gbr. Schmid)	–	1924-1967	–	125
Greppert & Kelch	Brandenburg	1912-1930	–	125
Gunthermann, S.G.	Nuremberg	1877-1965	Sigfried Gunthermann	126, 132
Hess, J.L.	Nuremberg	1826-1944	Mathias Hess	127-129
Heyde	Dresden	1872-1945	Georg Heyde	130-131
Horndlein	–	–	–	131
Issmayer	Nuremberg	1861-1933/34	J.A. Issmayer	132
Kellermann, Georg G. & Co.	Nuremberg	1910-1979	Georg Kellermann	49, 133

Early 700 Series, 1920.
Rear: (A-7) 9″. Middle: (A-60) 8″.
Front, left to right: (A-63) 7″, (A-62) 6″.

700 and 750 Series liners, 1920's.
Rear: (A-57) 14″ #750/7. Middle (A-52) 12″ #700/5.
Front, left to right: (A-9) 6″ #700/000, (A-8) 7″ #700/00,
(A-34) 8″ #700/0, (A-33) 8″ #700/1, (A-35) 9″ #700/2, (A-36) 10″ #700/3.
The 700 series was powered by an inertia motor which was cranked from
the stern. The 750 series utilized a clockwork motor which was wound
sometimes through the stern or sometimes through the stack.
Otherwise, both series were identical.

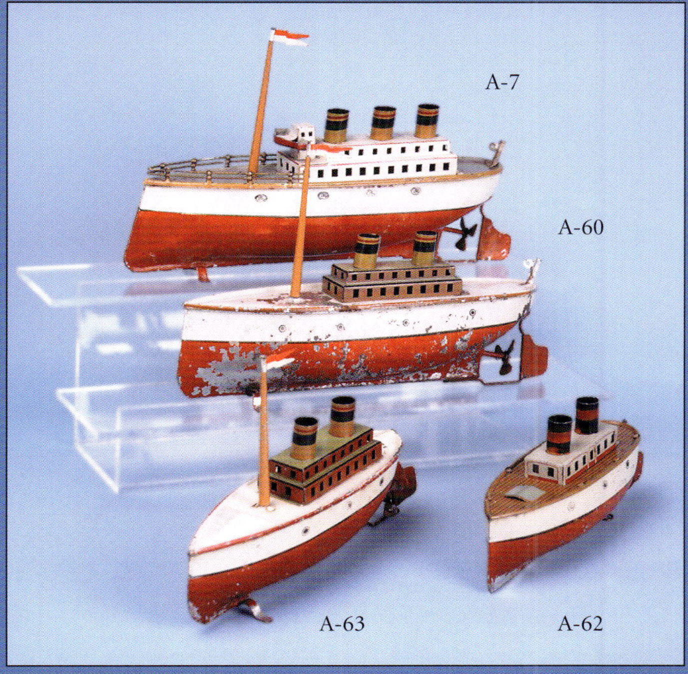

NAME	LOCATION	DATES	FOUNDER	PAGE
Kellner	Leipzig	–	Georg Kellner, Jr.	134
Lehmann, Ernst, Co.	Nuremberg	1881 to date	Ernst P. Lehmann	135
Levy, Georg (GELY)	Nuremberg	1921-1971	Georg Levy	134
Märklin, Gebrüder	Goppingen	1859 to date	Theo. Märklin	136-155
Meier, Johan Phillip	Nuremberg	1879-1917	Johan P. Meier	156
Mohr & Krauss (WK & MK)	Nuremberg	1895-1938	Wilhelm Krauss	156
Oro-Werke (Orobr)	Brandenburg	1908-1930's	Reil, Blechschmidt & Müller	157
Plank, Ernst	Nuremberg	1866-early 20thC	Ernst Plank	158-159
Reil & Co.	Brandenburg	1892-1908	Fritz Reil	157, 160
Richter	–	–	–	161
Rock & Graner (+ R&GN)	Biberach	1813-1904	C. Rock & G. Graner	162-163
Rosenbauer, Karl (KRN)	Nuremberg	1900-?	Karl Rosenbauer	164
Schoenner	Nuremberg	1875-1912	Jean Schoenner	165-166
Schuco	Nuremberg	1912 to date	Muller & Schreyer	167
Spenkuch	–	–	–	167
Staudt	Nuremberg	1860-1928	Leonard Staudt	168-170
Trix	Nuremberg	1927 to date	S. Bing & Oppenheimer	170
Uebelacker	Nuremberg	1860-?	Leonard Uebelacker	171-173
Unknown	various	–	–	174-175

1867–1919 & 1933–1935

Left to right:
(A-61) **1930's, 10″ liner;**
(A-79) **1930's, 8″ liner;**
(A-64) **1930's, 7″ liner.**
For a brief period this common
series of inertia-driven ships
was given quite colorful
paint schemes.

66

Series of liners from the late
1930's, which appears to be the
precursor to the 2025 series.
Clockwise from the left rear:
(A-56) **14″**, (A-49) **12″**,
(A-71) **11″**, (A-6) **9″**, (A-37) **11″**.
All are clockwork driven except A-37,
which has an inertia mechanism.

Arnold, Co.

1950's #2025 series is probably the best known and most popular of Arnold's liners.
Rear: (A-38) 16″ #2025/42.
Middle row, left to right:
(A-4) 13″ #2025/34,
(A-53) 12″ #2025/31,
(A-3) 11″ #2025/28,
(A-66) 9″ #2025/22.
Front, left to right:
(A-2) 8″ #2025/20,
(A-1) 6″ #2025/16.
All boats have clockwork motors.

2020 Series, 1950's.
Rear, left to right:
(A-11) 14″ #2020/36
was sold by FAO Schwarz in 1950,
(A-51) 11″ #2020/30,
(A-54) 8″ #2020/21,
(A-55) 6″ #2020/16.
Front: (A-15) 10″ #2020/25.

2000 Series, 1950's.
Rear: (A-10) 18″.
Middle row, left to right:
(A-12) 12″ #2085, (A-14) 8″ #2080,
(A-13) 12″ #2065.
Front, left to right: (A-44) 8″, (A-16) 12″ #2010.

Rear: (A-47) 1920's, 7″ #1201.
Front: (A-67) 1920's-30's, 6″ #1200.
**Both boats are clockwork driven.
Paddle-wheelers are cataloged
in 5 sizes.**

(A-59) Detail: The word "FOREIGN" that
appears at the waterline is an interesting
mark for a German toy. Export, no doubt!

Rear: (A-80)
1920's-30's, 8″ #1644 clockwork liner.
Front: (A-59)
1920's-30's, 9″ #1627, spring motor floor toy.

(A-5) Set from the 1930's. The clockwork powered hull is 7″ long and accommodates the two other ship superstructures.

A-5

69

Left to right:
(A-73) 1960's, 10″ liner,
(A-74) 10″ excursion boat.
Both are clockwork.

A-73

A-74

Clockwork powered
warships from the 1920's.
Left to right:
(A-65) 12″, (A-30) 10″.

1920's and 1930's warships
utilizing the same hull stamping.
Left to right: (A-68) 9″,
(A-70) 9″ #600/2, (A-48) 9″.
All are clockwork. The boat on the
right has a captain that pops up
from the bridge to take a look.

Rear: (A-18) **1950's, 10″ #2070.**
Front, left to right:
1920's & 30's, (A-69) **10″,** (A-42) **8″,**
(A-83) **8″,** (A-46) **10″ #1645,** (A-45) **8″.**
All are clockwork powered.

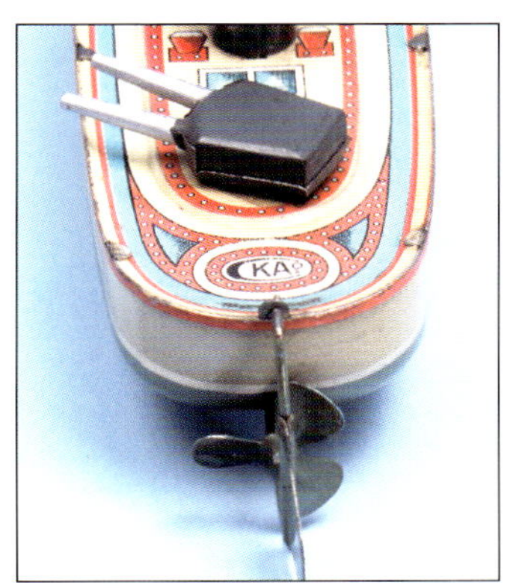

(A-83) This KA Co. trademark is unusual for a pre-1940 Arnold.

A-18

A-69   A-42   A-83   A-46   A-45

#2000 series clockwork diving submarines from the 1920's and 1930's.
Front to back:
(A-22) 6″ #2000, (A-23) 7″ #2001,
(A-24) 8″ #2002, (A-32) 9″ #2003.
These boats are often mistaken for those of other manufacturers. Their distinctively shaped rudder immediately identifies them.

A-32

A-24

A-23

A-22

A-20

Arnold, Co.

(A-20) 1938, 12″.
Note the differences in decoration
between this submarine and the
one made after 1946.

Submarines made after WW II.
Front to rear:
(A-21) 10″ #2004
sold at FAO Schwarz 1952-56,
(A-31) 7″ #2001, (A-19) 12″.
Although clockwork like the
others, this sub does not dive.

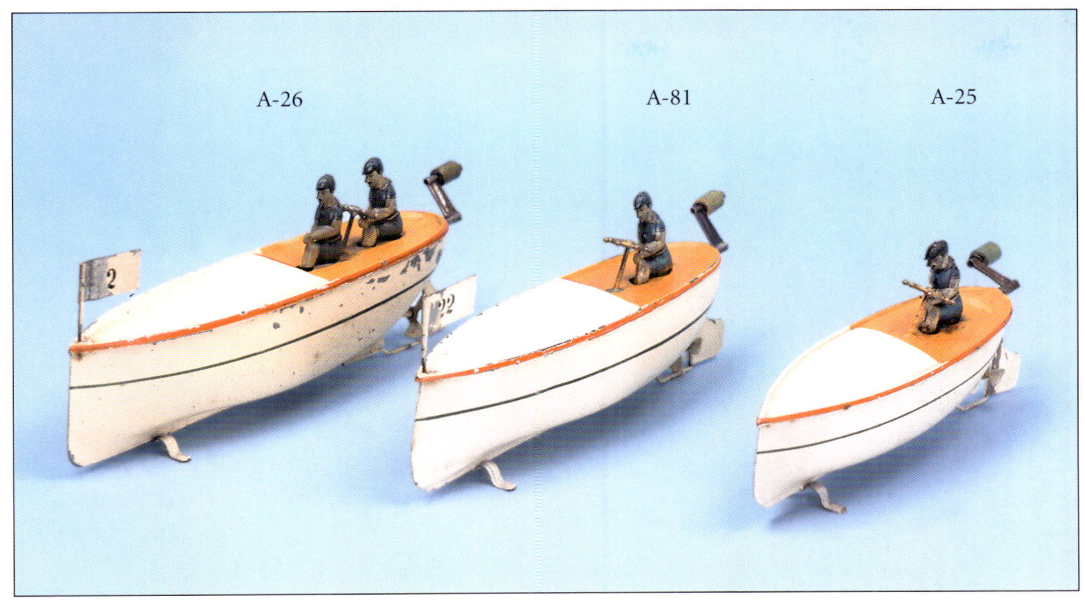

Left: (A-26) **1920, 8″ #1000/2.**
Middle: (A-81) **1920, 7 3/4″ #1000/1.**
Right: (A-25) **1920, 7″ #1000/0.**
An inertia motor that is cranked from the stern drives these speedboats. Arnold cataloged them in three sizes and clockwork versions in four. For some strange reason they are often misidentified as being made by Bing. It is unusual, however, to find a Bing toy without a trademark. Arnold products, on the other hand, were not widely trademarked until after WW II.

Left to right:
(A-78) **1920's-30's, 10″ #1601**
inertia motor airboat;
(A-28) **1920's-30's, 8″ #1600**
inertia motor airboat;
(A-29) **1920's-30's, 8″ #1625**
clockwork motor outboard motorboat.

Rear: (A-50) **1950's, 8″ #2030 rowboat and its colorful box.**
Middle row, left to right: (A-41) **1920's, 9″ #1611 two man rowboat;** (A-39) **1920's, 8″ #1612, Indian canoe.** Front: (A-77) **1920's, 8″ #1610 one man rowboat.**

1950's-60's speedboats. Clockwise from rear: (A-58) **11″ #1930,** (A-17) **5″ #2035, (A-76) 7″, (A-75) 6″.**

74

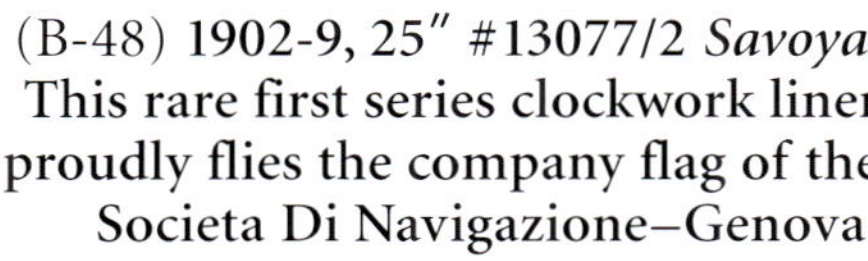

(B-48) 1902-9, 25″ #13077/2 *Savoya*.
This rare first series clockwork liner
proudly flies the company flag of the
Societa Di Navigazione–Genova.

B-48

Clean lines and lack of railing detail distinguish the 1912 series II liners. Some came with steam power but most were clockwork.
Back: (B-91) 39″ #155/350.
Middle: (B-12) 32″ #155/344.
Front, left to right:
(B-56) 10″ #155/324,
(B-95) 12″ #155/325,
(B-46) 20″ steam #155/352,
(B-109) 25″ #155/343.

Rear:(B-78) 1915, 8″ #155/333 with its original box.
Front:(B-112) mid-20's, 4″.

Gebrüder Bing

New in 1915, and made until 1927, the third series (Imperator) liners are widely found because of their lengthy production life.
Back: (B-61) **40″ #10/334/16.**
Third row: (B-79) **25″ #155/393.**
Second row, left to right:
(B-52) **16″ #155/391 or #10/334/12,**
(B-84) **20″ #155/392.**
Front: (B-105) **12″ #10/334/9.**

1914-15. Eleven sizes were cataloged for this intermediate series liner. Note the mixed characteristics between 4-stacked series II and 3-stacked series III.
Top to bottom:
(B-38) **20″ #155/338,**
(B-4) **14″ #155/336,**
(B-11) **12″ #155/335.**
All boats are powered by clockwork motors.

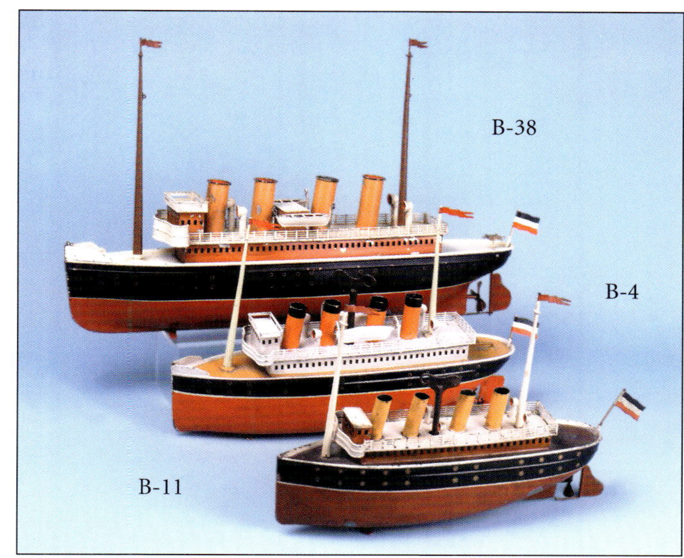

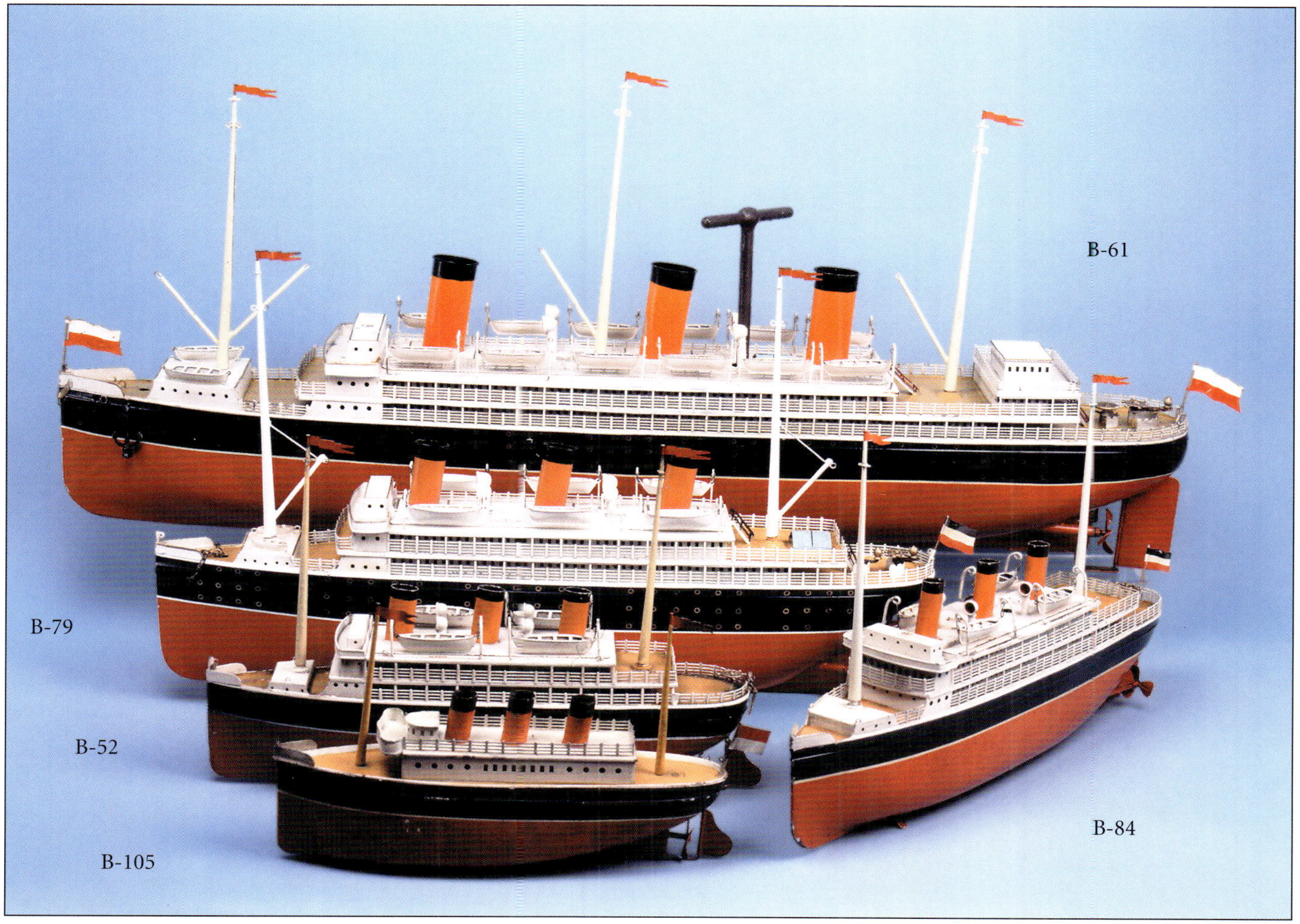

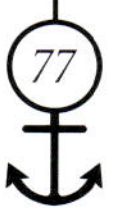

1923-27. These two are the largest and third largest *Leviathan* liners.
Back: (B-5) 39″ #10/334/16.
Front: (B-41) 25″ #10/334/14.

Leviathan 1923-27.
Left to right: (B-49) 20″ #10/334/13, (B-100) 14″ #10/334/10, (B-6) 12″ #10/334/9.
Front: (B-101) 8″.
Launched in 1913 as the Hamburg-America liner *Vaterland,* the ship was renamed *Leviathan* in 1917 following seizure by the U.S. Navy for use as a troop transport. When put back into trans-Atlantic passenger service by United States Lines, the ship was advertised as the world's largest ocean liner. Bing often accurately gave their version the US Line's characteristic red, white and blue stacks. These series III liners are mostly found nameless and with red and black stacks.

1927.
Left side, top to bottom:
(B-39) **13″ #10/333/8,**
(B-90) **10″ #10/333/7.**
Right side, top to bottom:
(B-62) **6″ #10/333/2,**
(B-57) **6″.**
All are clockwork.

1928-1931. The distinctive copper hulls make the last major series (IV) of Bing clockwork liners readily identifiable.
Back:
(B-7) **16″ #10/341/7.**
Front, left to right:
(B-116) **14″ #10/341/6,**
(B-77) **13″ #10/341/5,**
(B-92) **10″ #10/341/4,**
(B-96) **9″ #10/341/3,**
(B-89) **6″ #10/341/1.**

1902-1906 steam powered torpedo boats.
Rear: (B-22) 15″ #13089/1.
Front: (B-110) 22″ #13089/2.
Clockwork versions were available.
The wheeled boat-stands shown
came at extra cost.

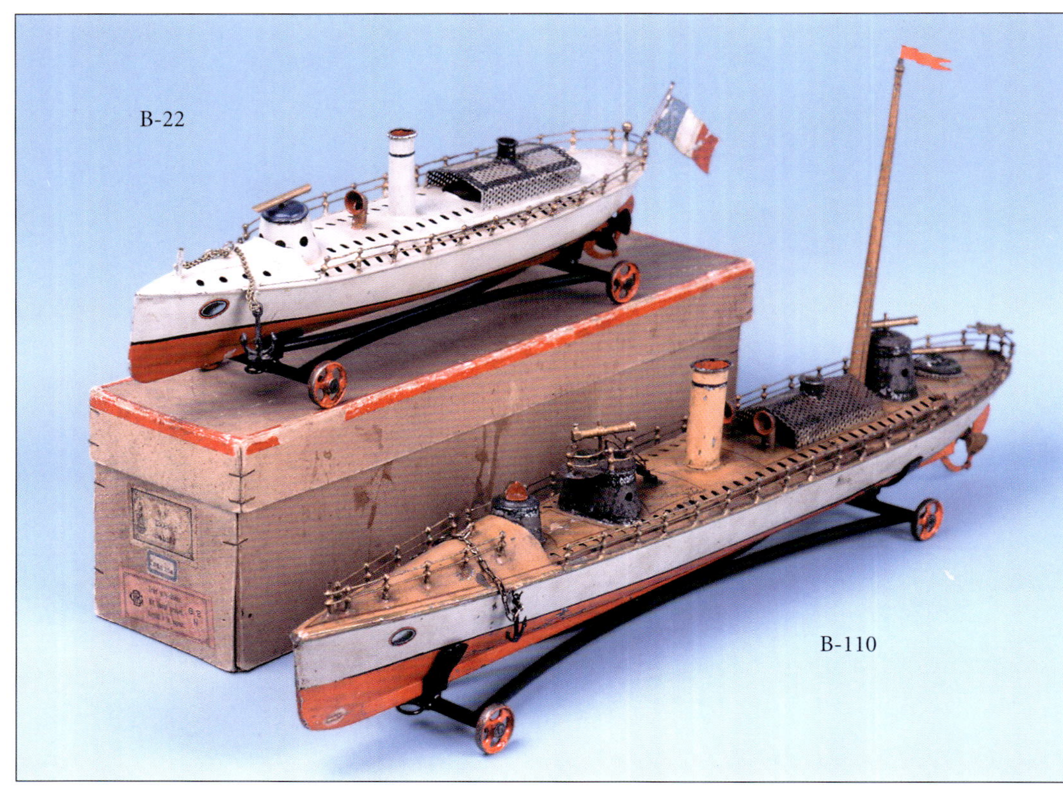

B-22

B-110

Foreground: (B-42) with box 1902-1909,
15″ clockwork, #13078/1 torpedo boat.
Back: (B-107) 19″ steam driven, probably
1902-1912. The wonderful graphics on the
box lid seem to depict the Kaiser reviewing
the fleet. At the turn of the 20th century
torpedo boats were very popular toys.
The advent of speedy turbine driven boats,
when combined with the improved Whitehead
torpedo, caused many naval strategists of the
time to believe that the day of the battleship
had passed. The revolutionary HMS
Dreadnought of 1906, along with the
development of torpedo boat destroyers
(later simply called destroyers), swung
the scales back in favor of the
battleship "battle-fleet."

B-107

B-42

B-83

B-19

1906-1909.
Rear: (B-83) 39″
#13957/2 or 155/162.
Front: (B-19) 28″
#13957/1 or 155/161.
This pair is clockwork
powered and was not
offered steam driven.

B-65

B-43

1906 clockwork
driven torpedo boats.
Left to right:
(B-65) 21″ #6868/4,
(B-43) 10″ #6868/1.
They came in four sizes.
Shown here are the
largest and smallest.

New destroyers in 1912, this three ship series came with steam or clockwork power.
Back:
(B-20) 39″ #155/553.
Middle:
(B-58) 28″ #155/152.
Front:
(B-60) 23″ #155/151.

Left side, top to bottom:
(B-21) 15″ #155/143,
(B-108) 10″ #155/141.
These are two of a 4-size 1912 clockwork series. The little (B-18) 8″ #10/342/2 on the right is one of a series of inexpensive boats made in the twilight of Bing production (1928).

1915-1928 clockwork torpedo boats.
Top to bottom:
(B-24) 21″ #155/231,
torpedo division boat;
(B-23) 15″ #155/223 or #10/343/3;
(B-8) 10″ #155/141 or #10/343/1.
This was the last series of Bing torpedo boat and
torpedo division boats. The largest was 39″ long and
was referred to as "Grosses Torpedo Divisions Boot."
It was also available with a steam engine.

Shown open

1904-1909.
Top pictures, left to right:
(B-17) **19″ #13804/3 or #155/93**,
(B-44) **15″ #13804/2 or #155/92**,
(B-87) **10″ #13804/1 or #155/91**.
Lower picture, top to bottom:
(B-120) **15″ #155/92**,
(B-44) **15″ #155/92**.
The one in the foreground has the later paint scheme. These cannon boats recall the Russo-Japanese War of 1904-5 and are often found with names like *Kasuga* or *Nowik* on their turrets. They contained a clockwork mechanism which not only powered the boat, but timed a lever which alternately fired a cap, then tripped the rudder to cause an 180 degree turn.

B-17   B-44   B-87

B-120

B-44

84

Shown open

B-13

B-73

B-45

This series of three "automatically firing gunboats" was new in 1912. They contain the same clockwork mechanism as the 1904-1909 series of #155/91 to #155/93 gunboats.
Top to bottom:
(B-13) 19″ #155/383,
(B-73) 15″ #155/382,
(B-45) 9″ #155/381.

1909-1912 armored cruisers.
Back: (B-64) 19″ #155/116.
Note the three propellers. Only the center one is operable.
Front, left to right:
(B16) 15″ #155/112,
(B-47) 12″ #155/111.
All are clockwork powered.

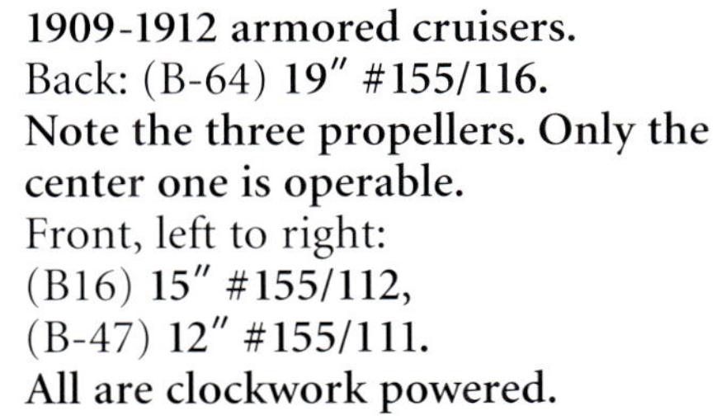

B-64 Detail

B-64

B-16

B-47

1912-1914
new armored cruiser series.
Top photo, rear to front:
(B-81) 36″ #155/446,
(B-104) 24″ #155/443.
Bottom right photo, left to right,
(B-75) 20″ #155/442,
(B-14) 17″ #155/441.
Bottom left photo:
(B-59) 28″ #155/444.
The unusual brown paint job
is entirely authentic. I am only the
second owner of the toy that was
originally purchased in France
by a wealthy American couple.
This could also account for the
overpainted trademark. All boats
are clockwork but certain sizes
could be purchased with steam.

Two of a series of three gunboats cataloged between 1902 and 1909.
Rear:
(B-85) 29″ #155/173, *King Edward,* is shown in a late color paint scheme with a built-in boat stand.
Front:
(B-103) 24″ #13080/2, *Massena,* has an early decal trademark and a typical-of-the-period inverted rudder. Both ships are clockwork, but could be purchased with a steam engine. Both were named for actual turn of the century pre-dreadnought battleships.

This 26″ clockwork "Dreadnought-type" battleship (B-102) #155/204 and it's larger 33″ sister were new in 1912. They had three propellers, two of which were only for show.

1914-15.
Shown are two of a series of three cage-masted armored ships for the American market. Left to right: (B-54) 19″ #155/126, (B-15) 16″ #155/125. They correspond to the similar, but tripod-masted series in the lower picture. The European versions were available with an optional selection of names.

Back: (B-80) 25 ″ #155/214.
Middle: (B-76) 19″ #155/126.
Front left: (B-97) 6″ #155/431.
Front right: (B-99) 12″ #155/724/2, *Leipzig.* All ships were cataloged as clockwork driven.

B-123

B-118

(B-123) 1902-09, 32″ #13082/3 battleship *Jaureguiberry.*
During the period of its production, this was Bing's largest warship. In its final cataloged year, under a new numbering system, it became #150/203. Various export destinations received appropriate names, such as *Furst Bismarck* and *HMS Terrible.* This particular ship was named for a former French Admiral and Minister of the Navy. Launched with great fanfare in 1893 during a Russian fleet visit to Toulon, it caused great anxiety at the British Admiralty, thus exacerbating an already heated naval expansion.

89

(B-118) 1902, 32″ *Kaiser Karl der Grosse.*
When the Blohm and Voss shipyard in Hamburg completed the *Kaiser Karl der Grosse* at the end of 1901, it was the last of a five ship pre-dreadnought Kaiser Frederich III class battleship. However, naval technology was advancing so rapidly that within five years it was totally obsolete. This formidable clockwork toy is a very realistic representation of the actual ship. Although un-cataloged, it was probably made between 1902 and 1905, and may be the only example.

1902-1912 .
Left to right:
(B-28) 16″ #13331/2 or #155/102,
(B-29) 11″ #13331/1 or #155/101,
(B-30) 9″ #13331/0 or #155/100.
When introduced, this series of clockwork submarines came in three sizes, 9″ to 27″. In 1906 there were four sizes and by 1909 there was an electric version of the largest sub available. In 1912 only the two smallest were cataloged.

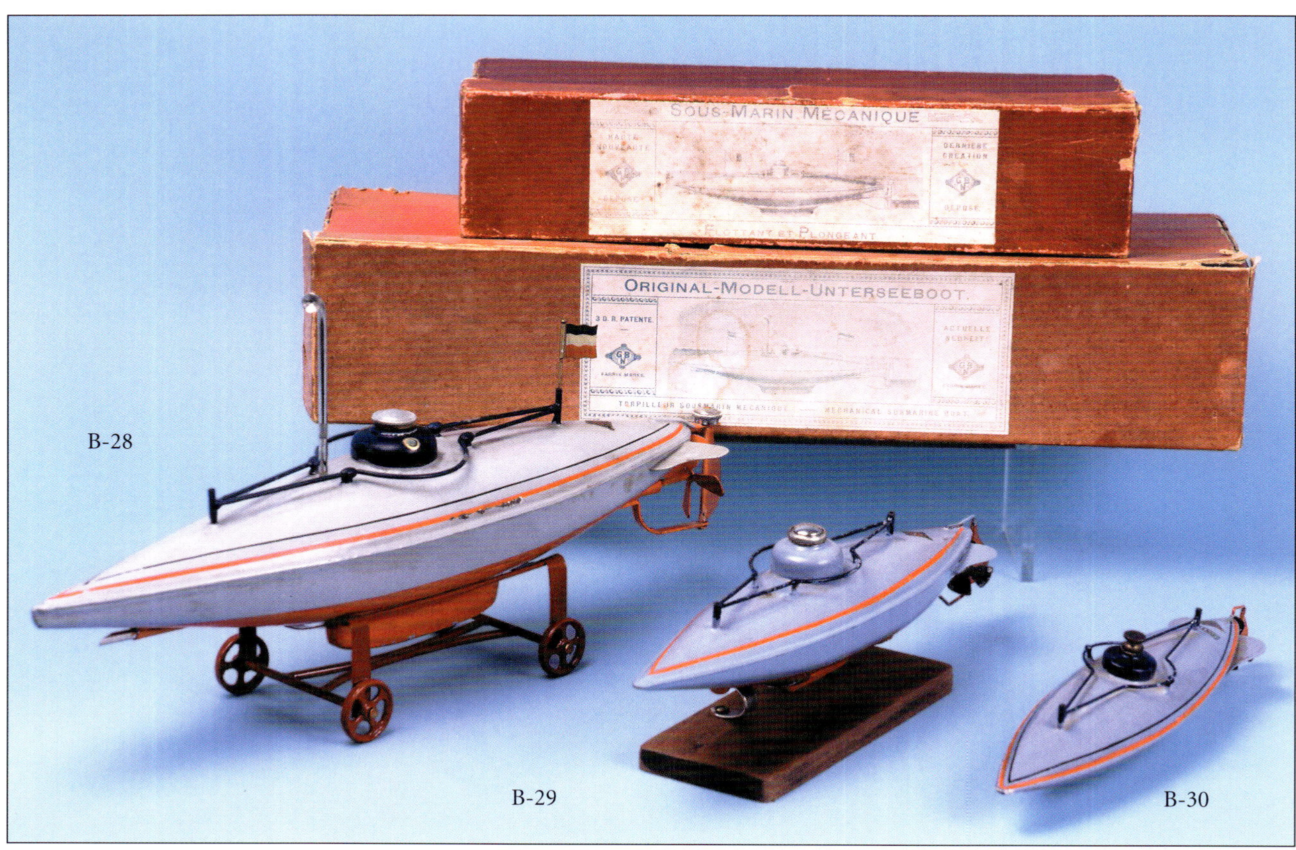

B-28

B-29

B-30

(B-28) **1912-15**

(B-29) **1906-12**

(B-30) **1902**

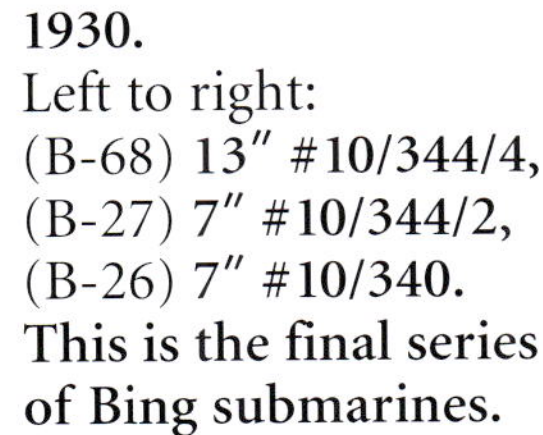

1912-27.
Top:
(B-86) **11″ #155/191 or #10/36/1.**
Middle:
(B-25) **9″ #155/190 or #10/36/0.**
Bottom left to right:
(B-72) **7″ #10/344/1,**
(B-70) **7″ #155/95,**
(B-94) **9″.**

1930.
Left to right:
(B-68) **13″ #10/344/4,**
(B-27) **7″ #10/344/2,**
(B-26) **7″ #10/340.**
**This is the final series
of Bing submarines.**

1915-1930.
Back:
(B-1) 20″ #10/39/2.
Front, left to right:
(B-2) 15″ #10/39/1, (B-3) 12″.
These clockwork American style paddle wheel ferry boats are quite realistic. The small *Union* is rather hard to find and was not cataloged by 1928.

By 1928-31 Bing was in serious financial trouble and their quality showed it. These clockwork driven ships are the last of their boats and are quite rare. Untypically, none carry the Bing trademark.
Back:
(B-82) 11″ #10/358.
Front, left to right:
(B-93) 10″ #10/359,
(B-69) 10″ #10/349.

Two 1913 fireboats. Left to right: (B-66) 12″ #155/603, (B-10) 9″ #155/602. In the background is an American style tug (B-9) 9″ #505/11/1, from about 1912, complete with an eagle on the pilothouse roof. All boats are clockwork powered. Fireboats were made in four sizes and tugboats in three.

This mid-1920's group of clockwork boats has similarly formed hulls. Back, left to right: (B-115) 8″ paddle-wheeler, (B-101) 8″ liner, (B-33) 8″ speed boat #10/337/3. Front, left to right: (B-114) 6″ liner, (B-117) 6″ fireboat, (B-112) 4″ liner, (B-98) 4″ speedboat.

(B-55) **19″**. Called a pinnace in 1902, this clockwork riverboat was numbered #13075/6. Under a new numbering system in 1909 it was #155/16. The figures on deck are specific to Bing, yet similar to other manufacturers.

The 1912 catalog shows three interchangeable, plate mounted, propulsion systems: clockwork, electric and steam. This electric boat, (B-36) 12″, contains the rarest of the systems. Unfortunately, the elaborately labeled original box no longer shows its catalog number.

German Manufacturers

B-37

B-35

The river steamers of 1913-14 came in three sizes. All were available with clockwork motors, but only one was cataloged as steam powered. Left to right: (B-37) 20″ #155/264, (B-35) 12″ #155/272 with steam plant.

95

B-111

B-74

B-34

A 1912 series of small clockwork paddle-wheelers. Top to bottom: (B-111) 10″ #155/363, (B-74) 8″ #155/362, (B-34) 7″ #155/361.

B-119

B-98

B-113

This group hails from the 1920's. Left to right: (B-119) 6″ with boathouse, (B-98) 4″, (B-113) 8″ floor toy. All are clockwork.

(B-53)
New in 1912, this 18″ sailboat, #155/312, had a mechanism that controlled the rudder in relation to the wind speed. It was cataloged in three sizes, the above being the smallest.

B-53

1909-1915.
Left to right:
(B-67) 10″ #155/23 or #155/26,
(B-50) 8″ #155/22 or #155/25,
(B-32) 6″ #155/21 or #155/24.
The second catalog number shown for these clockwork speedboats is the result of a 1915 renumbering system.

B-67

B-50

B-32

B-63

B-106

1927.
Left to right:
(B-63) 23″ #10/360
steam powered,
(B-106) 23″ #10/329
clockwork powered.
Produced throughout
the 20's, these were the
last racing boats of
quality construction.

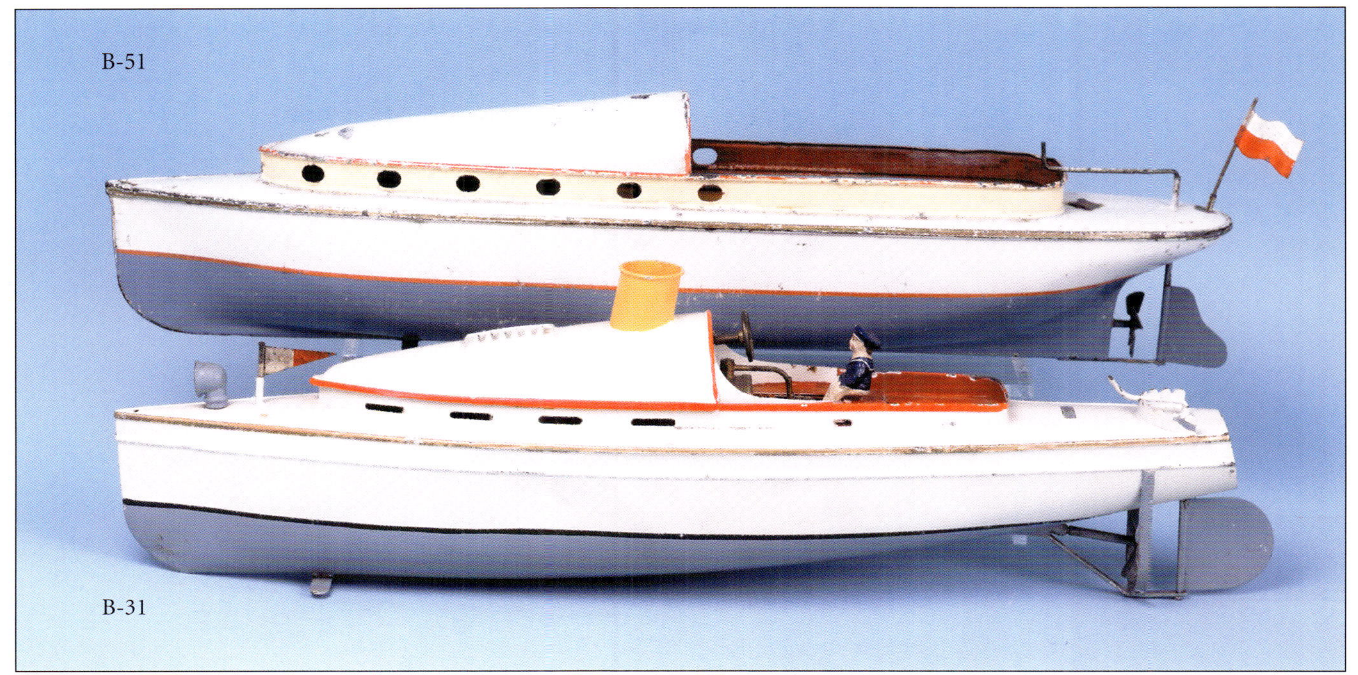

B-51

B-31

Back:
(B-51) 1909-12, 19″
#155/33. 33 series
clockwork racing boat
was cataloged in 4 sizes,
10″ to 23″.
Front:
(B-31)1912, 18″
#155/35 steam powered
racing boat came in
two sizes.

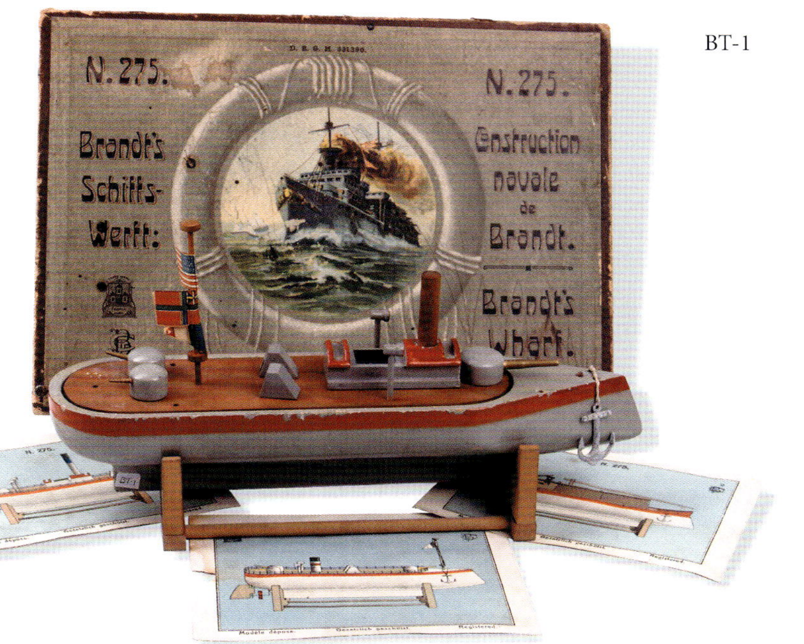

BT-1

(BT-1) This wooden boat building set from about 1900 contained colorful prints as guidance in assembling various configurations. The hull is 13″ long.

Even though the canopy was replaced while they were permanently soldered to the deck, this original romantic couple continues to enjoy a musical interlude.

Büchner

The three boats clockwise from the left are by Büchner: (BH-3) 4″ nonpowered pinnace, (BH-1) 7″ clockwork paddle-wheeler, (BH-2) 4″ nonpowered pinnace. They date from as early as 1850. The two 4″ boats in the foreground are probably by Issmayer and probably from around 1900.

C-13

(C-13) **1905, 8″ #712/1.** This clockwork ship was available in six sizes. The Butler Brothers catalog of 1905 offered the 11″ version.

C-23

F-69

Left:
(C-23) **1911, 12″ #713/24.** The 713 series came in an incredible 19 sizes from 7″ to 30″ long. Right: (F-69) **1930,** Fleischmann 11″ liner. This illustrates the close similarity of the products of the two manufacturers. After George Carette left Germany, his tooling was disseminated throughout Nuremberg, possibly accounting for the likeness. However, it is more probable that Fleischmann made the boats for Carette all along.

All are from 1914.
Rear: (C-2) 10″ #732/24.
Middle: (C-24) 9″ #732/23.
Front: (C-1) 8″ #732/21.
An incredible 13 sizes,
up to 20″ (#732/32),
were cataloged for this
clockwork driven series.
Interestingly, the 1915 Märklin
catalog displays what are
obviously Carette boats
(7 liners and 7 warships).
They are listed as "simple models
at a fair price-range."

100

All are shown in the 1914
(final year for Carette) catalog.
Rear: (C-21) 14″ #734/26.
Middle: (C-3) 12″ #732/27.
Front: (C-4) 10″#734/24.
Even when original boxes
are present, the lack of a
trademark makes positive
attribution difficult.

Rear:
(C-25) **1911, 13″ #737/13A,** clockwork cruiser.
Front:
(F-96) **1908, 6″.** While easily mistaken for Carette, this small clockwork gunboat is shown as part of a set in the Fleischmann catalog.

Carette/Fleischmann, or the "Your Guess Is As Good As Mine Department!"
Rear:
(C-26) **18″ battleship.**
Front, left to right:
(UK-60) **11″ tug,**
(FK-2) **14″ battleship,**
(C-27) **16″ battleship.**
All boats are clockwork.

(C-20) 1914, 14″ # 714/? This uniquely styled warship is shorter than those listed at 49cm, 53cm and 60cm in Carette's 1914 catalog. The clockwork ship has been totally restored.

C-20

Rear: (C-19) 16″.
Front: (C-5) 10″.
Clockwork torpedo boats. Pictured in the Universal Toy Catalog, 1924/1926, these two display the Carette style in spite of the fact that the company no longer existed. Fleischmann again is the possible alternative.

C-19

C-5

The ship on the left (C-7) 1900's, 18″, cannot be found in any Carette catalog and was probably made by Fleischmann. The riverboat on the right (C-18) 16″, is found in Carette's 1905 catalog, once more showing the similarities of the manufacturers. Both are clockwork.

(C-8) 1900, 13″ steam powered riverboat. One of the factors in the difficulty in the identification of Carette boats, other than lack of trademark and sparse catalogs, is their seeming penchant for purchasing from other manufacturers. In this case, what appears to be a Schoenner product is found in a Carette box.

(C12) **1911, 6″ #717/1R.** This inertia driven, lithographed floor toy is quite similar in construction to those boats produced by Hess. In fact in the 1911 Carette catalog, this boat is shown next to a torpedo boat that is definitely of Hess heritage. Therefore, in spite of the G.C.Co trademark, its true manufacturer is in question. This "Saloon steamer with deck" was also available in a spring driven version.

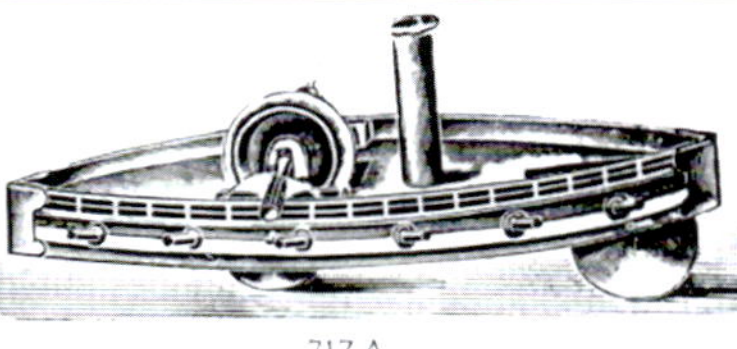

Salondampfer mit Verdeck.

No. 717/1 R mit Rollerantrieb, 17 cm lang, Dutzend M. 4.45
— 717/1 U — Uhrwerk, 17 — — — — 5.55

Torpedoboot.

— 717 A mit Rollerantrieb, 24 cm lang, Dutzend — 4.50

Rear: (C-32) 1914, 12″ #736/25, riverboat.
Front: (C-22) 1914, 7″ #731/21, riverboat. Nine sizes of this clockwork series were cataloged.

104

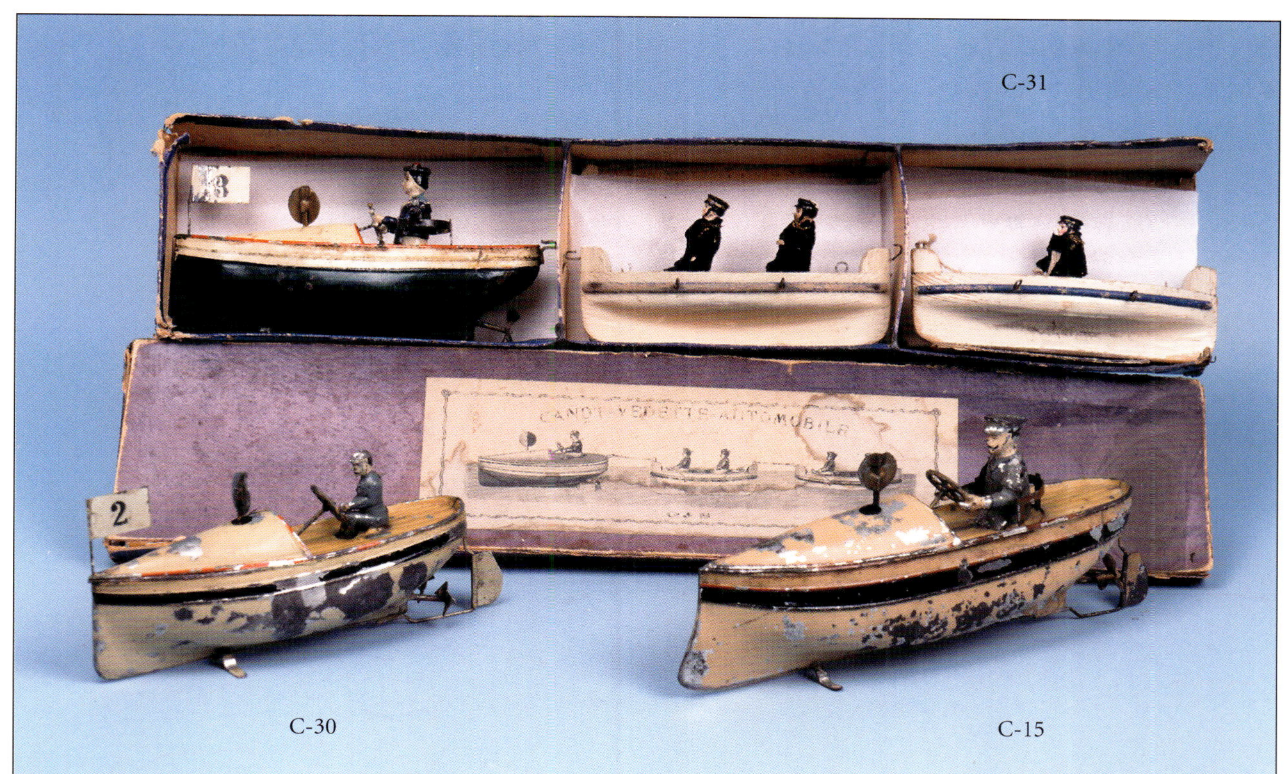

C-31

C-30

C-15

Clockwork speedboats.
Front row, left to right:
(C-30) **1905, 7″ #719/2;**
(C-15) **10″ #719/4.**
Rear set: (C-31).
The speedboat towing the two wooden boats has all the traits of its companions on the front row, but the box is marked "G & S."

C-29

C-22

C-17

Back row:
(C-29) **1914, 7″ #725/20, yacht;**
(C-22) **1914, 7″ riverboat.**
Front: (C-17) **6″ unknown, but has Carette/Fleischmann characteristics. It is not true that only Carette had smoke imitating wind-up keys.**

All these 4″ penny toys
are from the 1920's.
Clockwise from the left rear:
(DR-2)
spring driven speedboat,
(DR-1)
spring driven liner,
(DR-3)
flywheel driven battleship.

Gebrüder Einfalt (Kosmos)

(ET-1) 1930-33,
14″ #193 *Bremen.*
As this spring driven
floor toy meanders
along its way, the
captain emerges from
the bridge.

FK-1

FK-4

FK-5

During the 1920's, Falk cataloged 10 of these liners ranging in size from 7″ to 23″.
From top to bottom:
(FK-1) 16″ #2022/7,
(FK-4) 12″ #2022/5,
(FK-5) 10″ #2022/4.
Also cataloged were six sizes of similarly configured paddle-wheelers.

107

FK-6

(FK-6) 20″ #193. Lacking catalogs to date this piece, one can only assume pre-WW I.

(FK-2) **14″**.
Several knowledgeable
"experts" have vetted this
warship, yet to me it has
many Fleischmann and
Carette features. The masts
do not appear to be original,
thus losing some means
of identification.

Fischer was quite a
prolific producer of
penny toys, nautical
types in particular.
Clockwise from
the upper right:
(FR-5) 6″,
(FR-3) 9″,
(FR-4) 4″,
(FR-1) 4″,
(FR-2) 7″ #48.

Rear: (F-58) 1930-36, 32″ #520/80.
Front: (F-16) 1930-36, 24″ #520/60.
Two of the largest Fleischmann clockwork liners, these sizes were discontinued after 1938. The *Kronprinzessin Cecilie* of 1907 was larger at 84″, but rather than being a toy it was a 1:100 scale model. In 1930 the 24″ ship was numbered #989 and the 32″ was #991. The "Spezial Katalog" shows a 40″ size but does not list its price.

F-58

F-16

Still included in the Fleischmann 1929 price list, this pre-WW I series of twenty "Pleasure Steamers" ranged in length from 17cm to 80cm. In 1911 they appear as the 713 series in Carette's catalog and some of them in Märklin's 1915 catalog. The boxed boats shown here are undoubtedly Fleischmann since the numbers correspond with those listed in their catalog. Although some Carette and Fleischmann cataloged boats appear to be identical, Carette's were offered with optional bow name inprints.
Clockwise from the left rear:
(F-107 w/box) 9″ #952, or Carette #713/22;
(C-23 w/box) 12″ #954, or Carette #713/24;
(F-95 w/box) 7″ #950, or Carette #713/20;
(F-64) 16″ #957; (F-69) 11″ #954;
(F-78) 7″ #951; (F-53) 10″ #953.

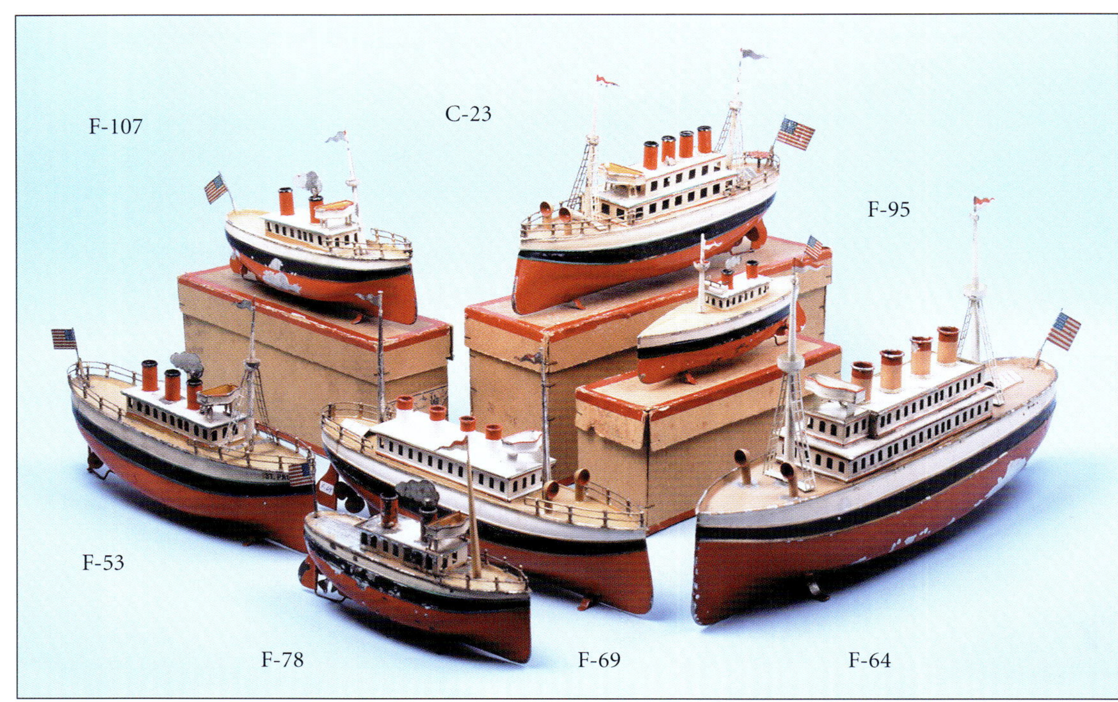

Foreground: (F-59) 1930, 13″ #984. The version in the back (F-13) has an unusual removable top which allows access to the battery compartment for the flashing light mechanism. Both ships are clockwork driven.

"Newest Pleasure Steamers" of 1930 included 12 sizes from catalog numbers 979 to 992.
Rear: (F-89) 19″ #988.
Middle, left to right: (F-74) 10″ #983, (F-56) 17″ #987.
Front, left to right: (F-65) 7″ #941 (this boat is from an earlier series), (F-59) 13″ #984.

In 1936 these clockwork ships were
the 510 & 520 series in eleven sizes.
In 1955 they were the 830 series
in eight sizes.
Rear: (F-90)19″ #520/50.
Middle, left to right:
(F-11) 10″ #510/27,
(F-12) 12″ #520/30,
(F-81) 13″ #520/33,
(F-14) 16″ #520/40.
Front, left to right:
(F-47) 8 5/8″ #510/22,
(F-8) 7″ #510/19,
(F-77) 7″ #510/16.

This very popular line of ships
was sold from 1935 to 1955.
In the 30's it was the 540 series
and in the 50's, the 830 series.
Rear: (F-15) 19″ #830/50.
Middle, left to right:
(F-80) 12″ #540/30,
(F-19) 13″ #830/33,
(F-18) 16″ #830/40,
(F-17) 17″ #830/45.
Front, left to right:
(F-87) 6″ #540/16,
(F-10) 7″ #540/19,
(F-85) 8″ #830/22,
(F-57) 10″ #830/27.

Both rear-wound inertia motors (F-9) #510/19R and through-the-stack key wound clockwork (F-8) #510/19 versions were available in the 7″ 510 series of 1936. (UK-56). In the center rear is an almost identical Japanese copy. (F-21) 1936, 4″ #F/300. The little launch in the foreground was produced until 1955.

112

Rear: (F-1)1950, 20″ #856. Front: (F-2) 1936, 20″ #526. The white version is probably the best known of all Fleischmann's clockwork boats. It was cataloged by FAO Schwarz in the early 1950's.

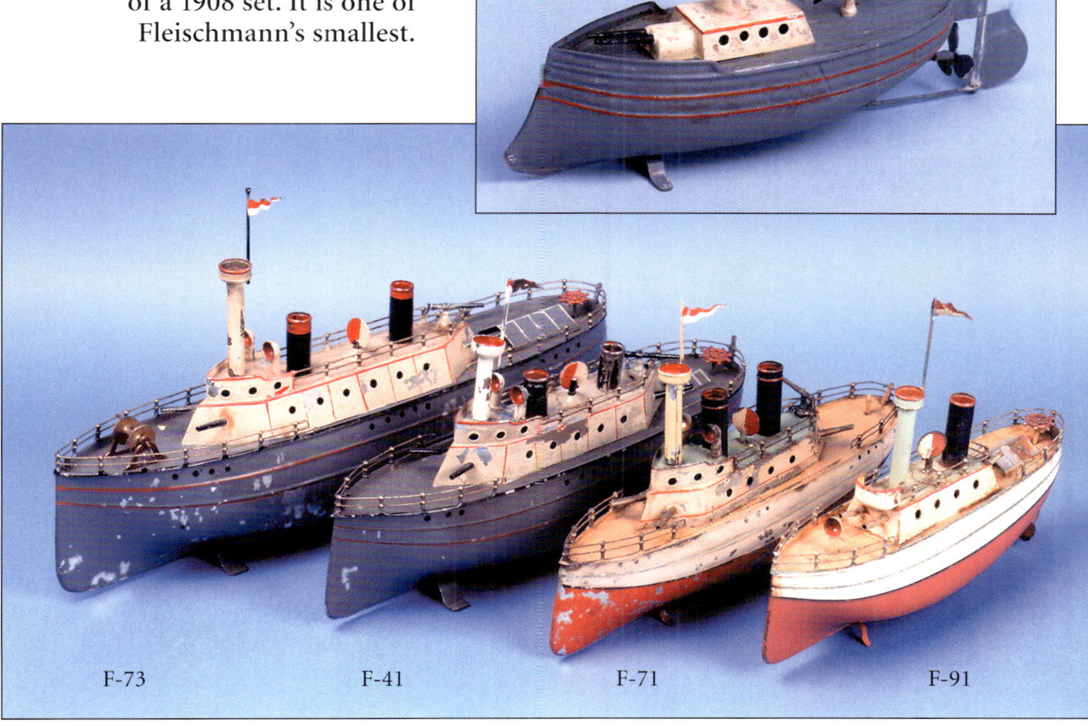

(F-96) 6″.
This diminutive clockwork warship can be found as part of a 1908 set. It is one of Fleischmann's smallest.

F-96

F-73   F-41   F-71   F-91

New in 1908, these coastal cruisers represent some of the 18 different ships cataloged as the 800 series. Since Fleischmann had not as yet applied a numbering system that indicated the length of the boat (i.e. 640/45 = 640 series x 45cm), it is difficult to determine how many ships of the series were of the same configuration.
Left to right: (F-73) 16″ #807,
(F-41) 13″ #805,
(F-71) 11″ #804,
(F-91) 10″ possibly Carette.

C-25

F-40

F-94   F-75

The 1908 coastal cruisers on the left came in 18 sizes, 7″ to 39″.
They are, top to bottom:
(C-25) 13″ #265, (F-94) 9″ #262.
The torpedo boats on the right were cataloged in 11 sizes, 7″ to 24″ (1930 had 8 sizes).
Top to bottom:
(F-40) 12″ #654,
(F-75) 9″ #652.
The two ships on the bottom utilize the same hull as the 9″ paddle-wheeler.

1936 saw a line of clockwork warships (#640) in ten sizes from 6″ to 29″. There were four sizes (#630) made with flywheel (inertia) propulsion.

Top right picture from top to bottom: (F-27) 20″ #640/52, (F-46) 17″ #640/45.

Lower right picture from top to bottom: (F-43) 14″ #640/36, (F-28) 13″ #630/33, (F-29) 10″ #630/27, (F-30) 7″ #630/19, (F-79) 6″ #630/16.

(F-54) 17″ #808.
This oddly configured clockwork warship was listed in 1930 along with 19 other ships of the 800 series. It has been partially restored.

F-60

F-26

In the back: (F-60) **19″ #527 is the version shown in the 1935/36 catalog supplement.** (F-26) **19″ #857** from 1955 is seen in the foreground.

F-31

F-48

F-51

A realistic group of 1955 clockwork driven destroyers. Left to right: (F-31) **15″ #870/39,** (F-48) **12″ #870/30,** (F-51) **9″ #870/23.**

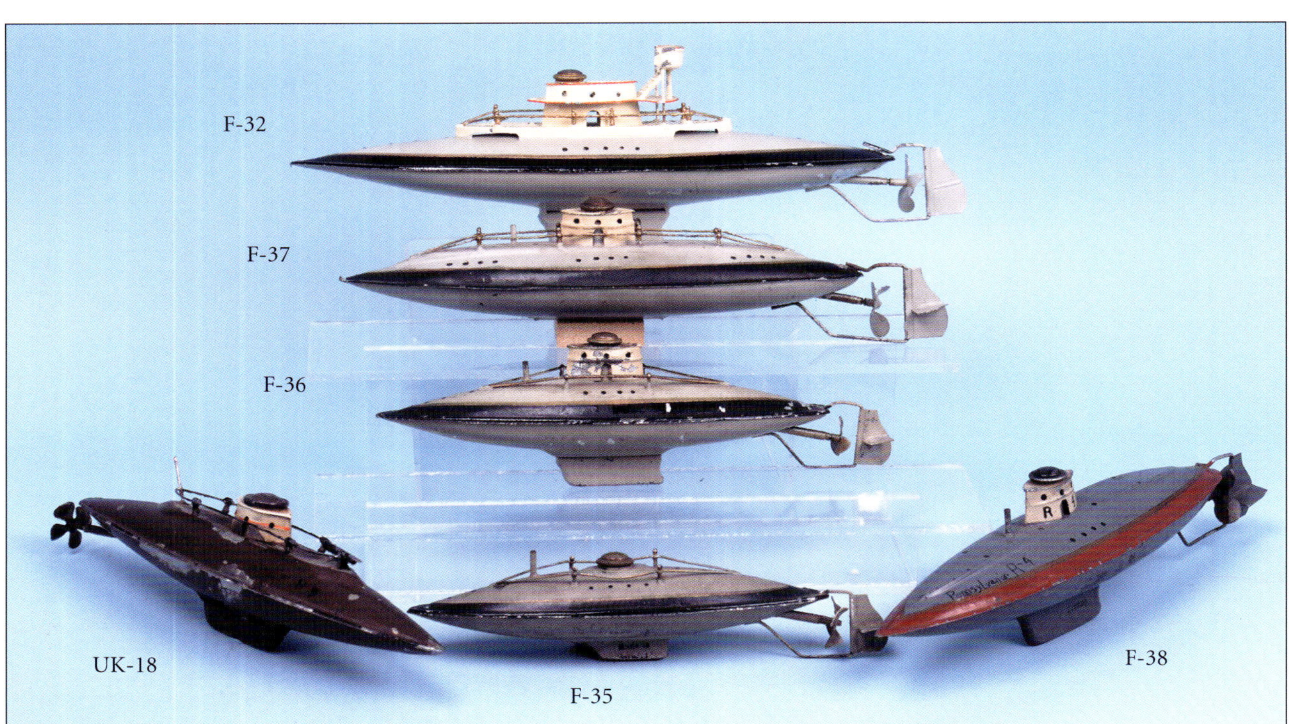

From the 1920's to the 30's, the 660 series clockwork submarine was very popular. They are still readily found by collectors. There were seven sizes offered from 7″ to 14″.
Top to bottom:
(F-32) 12″ #66/30,
(F-37) 10″ #660/27,
(F-36) 8″ #660/22,
(F-35) 7″ #660/20.
Right: (F-38) 10″ #660/25.
Left: (UK-18) 9″.
This boat is found labeled as manufacturer #116 in *The Universal Toy Catalog 1924/1926*.

In 1901 Fleischmann patented this style of clockwork submarine. They were listed for sale in five sizes until 1930. An example like the one on the left is also shown in the Carette catalog.
Top: (F-109) 11¼″ #153
Bottom, left to right:
(F-66) 7″ #150,
(F-67) 8″ #151,
(F-68) 7″.

Left to right:
(F-36) 8″ #600/22,
(UK-17) 8″ Japanese copy
of Fleischmann's
1936 #600/22.

"Latest Novelty" of 1936,
these variants of the 13″
#670/35 submarine are
one of three sizes
introduced that year.
On the left (F-33) is a
U-boat style, apparently
for the German market,
while on the right (F-34)
is an American design.

Nine sizes of these clockwork ferryboats were cataloged in 1908. There were still three sizes in 1930. Left: (F-61) 19″ #457 (hull has been restored). Right: (F-25) 13″ #454.

1936-1955 "Special Value, Durable Construction," this line of inexpensive clockwork ships was quite popular and may still be readily found today. Back: (F-86) 10″ #820. 3rd row, left to right: (F-93) 7″ #530/18, (F-7) 10″ #322, (F-6) 8″ #530/21. 2nd row, left to right: (F-20) 7″ #310, (F-105) 7″ #311. Front, left to right: (F-20C) 7″ #331, (F-20A) 7″ #330, (F-20B) 7″ #332.

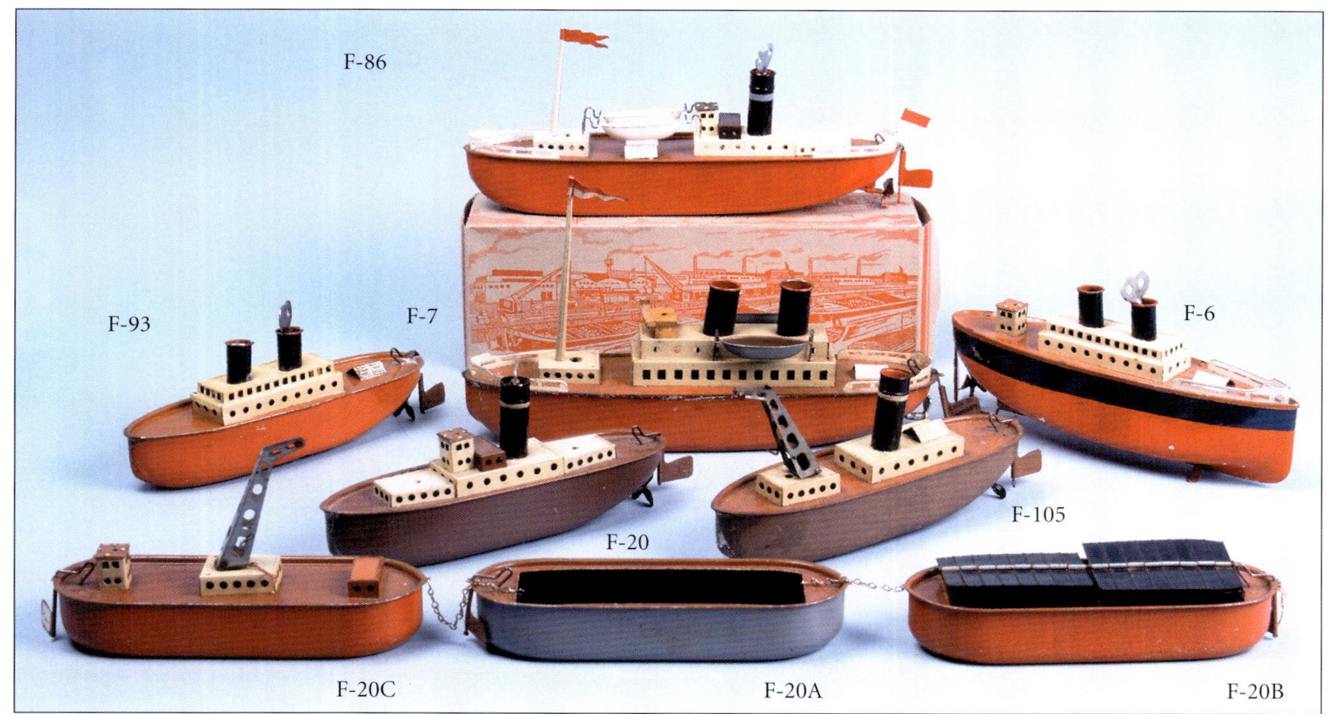

Rear to front:
(F-3) 1936, 20″ #525;
(F-4) 1955, 20″ #855;
(F-5) 1955, 15″ #860/39.

Eight sizes of clockwork houseboats
were listed in the 1908 catalog.
Foreground: (F-42) 6″ #470, the smallest.
Rear: (F-23) 8″.
This boat, due to its details and dimensions,
cannot be positively attributed to Fleischmann.

Shown are clockwork fireboats that have an internal
pump to spray a stream of water from the forward
mounted nozzle. Oddly, both have the same catalog
number. In 1908 the top boat (F-45) 11″ was #511
and in 1930 (F-22) 10″ on the bottom was #511.
Eight sizes were shown in 1908, but by 1930
there were only three.

In 1908 Fleischmann cataloged 14 sizes of paddle-wheelers.
There were still 11 sizes listed in 1930.
Shown clockwise from the left front:
(F-63) 13″ #74R, (F-50) 16″ #75R,
(F-52) 19″ #77R, (F-84) 10″ #79R,
(F-104) 10″ #79R – early, (F-88) 7″ #70R.
These ships, like their ocean liner cousins,
are often mistaken for those marketed by Carette.

Left to right: (F-106) 4″ 1908, (F-101) 4″.
Both boats are nonpowered even though the one
on the right displays the smoke fixture usually
used for clockwork winding.

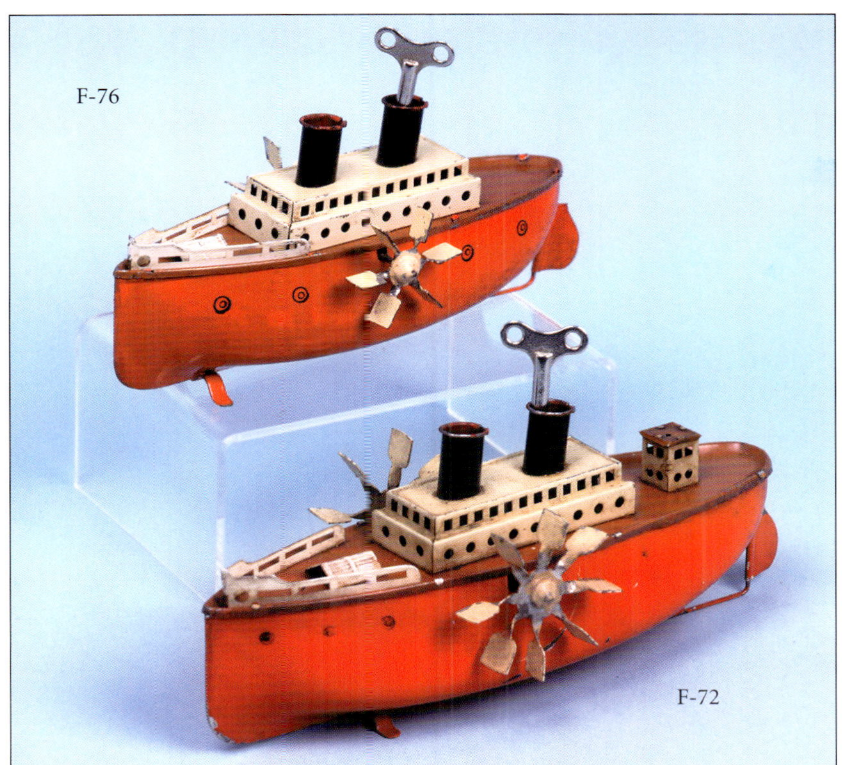

F-76

F-72

Two of a series of four, ranging in size from 6″ to 9″, these 1936 paddle-wheelers are latecomers to the Fleischmann line.
Top: (F-76) 7″ #750/18.
Bottom: (F-72) 8″ #750/21.

F-49

F-83

The 1908 catalog includes these two early paddle-wheelers.
Top: (F-49) 13″ #26R. Bottom: (F-83) 7″ #13R. Note that the key port is just behind the paddle wheel rather than through the stack. A child must have cruelly blinded the figures seated at their table, for they are otherwise in excellent condition.

121

Left to right:
(F-24) 1908, 12″ #704;
(FK-3) 1900, 8″.
Both boats are clockwork.
The one on the right can be
found in the 1900 Ullmann
and Engelmann catalog. Since
distributors did not publicize
the manufacturer's name, it
is difficult to positively attribute
the source. Its similarity to the
Fleischmann on the left, however,
is a fairly convincing argument.

The rear vessel is a 1908
clockwork passenger steamer that
came in 15 sizes from 9″ to 33″.
This one (F-62) 16″ #604
has been restored with a
stack mistakenly added.
In 1930 the series, by then
down to 9 sizes, was offered
as a pleasure steamer.
Foreground:
(F-55) 7″ #901, is one of a
series new in 1908, also called
pleasure steamers, which were
offered in an amazing
18 sizes from 7″ to 31″.

F-70

Gebrüder Fleischmann

(F-70) 6″. An innovative way of concealing the key port in this 1908 sailboat. This clockwork powered series of boats was offered in seven sizes, from 6″ to 16″. Note how the jib boom hooks into the bowsprit.

F-99

(F-99) 10″ #854. Carried by FAO Schwarz in 1954. This excursion steamer is rarely found intact due to its brittle plastic hull.

The two 6″ & 10″ diameter lighthouse ponds are often attributed to Fleischmann but cannot be found in any catalog. Falk would be another possibility.

Gebrüder Fleischmann

1908 sets.
Left to right: (F-103) 5″, (F-102) 6″, (F-101) 4″, (F-97) 3″, (F-98) 3″.
The castle (F-82) and pond of 7″ diameter, shown here with a 3″ boat, often came with a swan. In 1908 it was cataloged as #127. Similar models came in 8 sizes. In 1930 it was still listed in the catalogs, but as #774.

In 1908 Fleischmann sold two dozen different sets of small magnetic toys. These were still being marketed throughout the 1920's. More often than not, they are found as individual items. The box on the left (F-100) retains its original excelsior.

Gescha (Gbr. Schmid)

(GR-1 & GR-2) **1950 7″.**
As they proceed forward,
these clockwork
floor toys tack.

Greppert & Kelch

1924-26.
Back: (GK-2) **11″ *Ocean*.**
Front, left to right:
(GK-1) **9″ *Express*,**
(UK-15) **6″, possibly G&K.**

GN-4

(GN-4) 1920's, 27″. Clockwork floor toy with eight oarsmen. Although no trademark appears on the shell, its original box attests to its manufacturer.

Front: (GN-1) 14″ single oarsman.
Rear, left to right: (GN-2) 18″ twin oarsmen with coxswain, (GN-4) 27″ 8-man crew with coxswain, (GN-3) 22″ 4-man skull with coxswain. The crews of these racing shells came with a variety of painted uniforms often representing Cambridge and Oxford Universities. Other manufacturers produced similar toys.

Flywheel powered
floor toys from the first
part of the 20th century.
Rear: (H-8) 12″.
Middle row, left to right:
(H-5) 6″,
(H-7) 9″,
(H-16) 9″.
Front, left to right:
(H-18) 4″,
(H-6) 7″.

The top photo shows
an early pre-WW I Hess
trademark. The lower is
a version from the 1920's.
These both appear on
the same boat! (H-16)

Rear group: (H-10) 9″ spring powered gunboat
with four 5″ nonpowered subs in tow.
Front, left to right: (H-9) 6″ flywheel powered sub,
(H-12) 9″ #13/1 spring powered destroyer.
All these floor toys are from about 1925.

(H-11) 1910.
While the pieces of this pre-WW I set are often found, rarely is it seen in the original box with all the towing bars and paper flags.

Two different 8″ spring driven battleships.
Left to right: (H-13), (H-11).
Note the drawbar post at the stern of the right-hand toy indicating that this ship was part of a set.

H-11

(H-1) 1920, 8″.
Unusual riverboat floor toy is flywheel driven, as are many Hess ships. The front wheel axle is off-center, thus giving the boat a rocking motion as it proceeds along its way.

(H-14) 1925, 12″ #11/3p.
Spring powered speedboat
floor toy.

J.L. Hess

Back: (UK-88) **10″**.
Front: (H-15) **3″**.
While neither of these flywheel driven ships have a trademark, both display all the characteristics of Hess.

Left to right:
(H-4) 6″ #1038,
(H-3) 9″ #1041,
(H-2) 11″ #1045.
All are flywheel driven and have cardboard sails. The 9″ & 12″ versions are shown in the 1905 John Wanamaker department store catalog.

(HE-1) *Sea Battle.* A late 19th Century set. Note the lead-cast puffs of smoke emanating from each ship's bow gun. The gray cotton smoke from the stacks is typical with Heyde sets.

HE-1

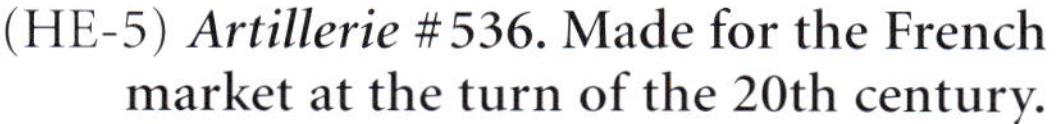

(HE-5) *Artillerie #536.* Made for the French market at the turn of the 20th century.

HE-5

HE-2

(HE-2) *American Fleet Parade* 1900.

HE-5

HE-3

Heyde

(HE-3) *Panzerflotte* of 1905 depicting a Japanese engagement with Russian torpedo boats. Admiral Togo destroyed the Russian fleet in a two day battle in the Strait of Tsushima during the Russo-Japanese War. The torpedo boats are each 5″ long while the battleship is 7″.

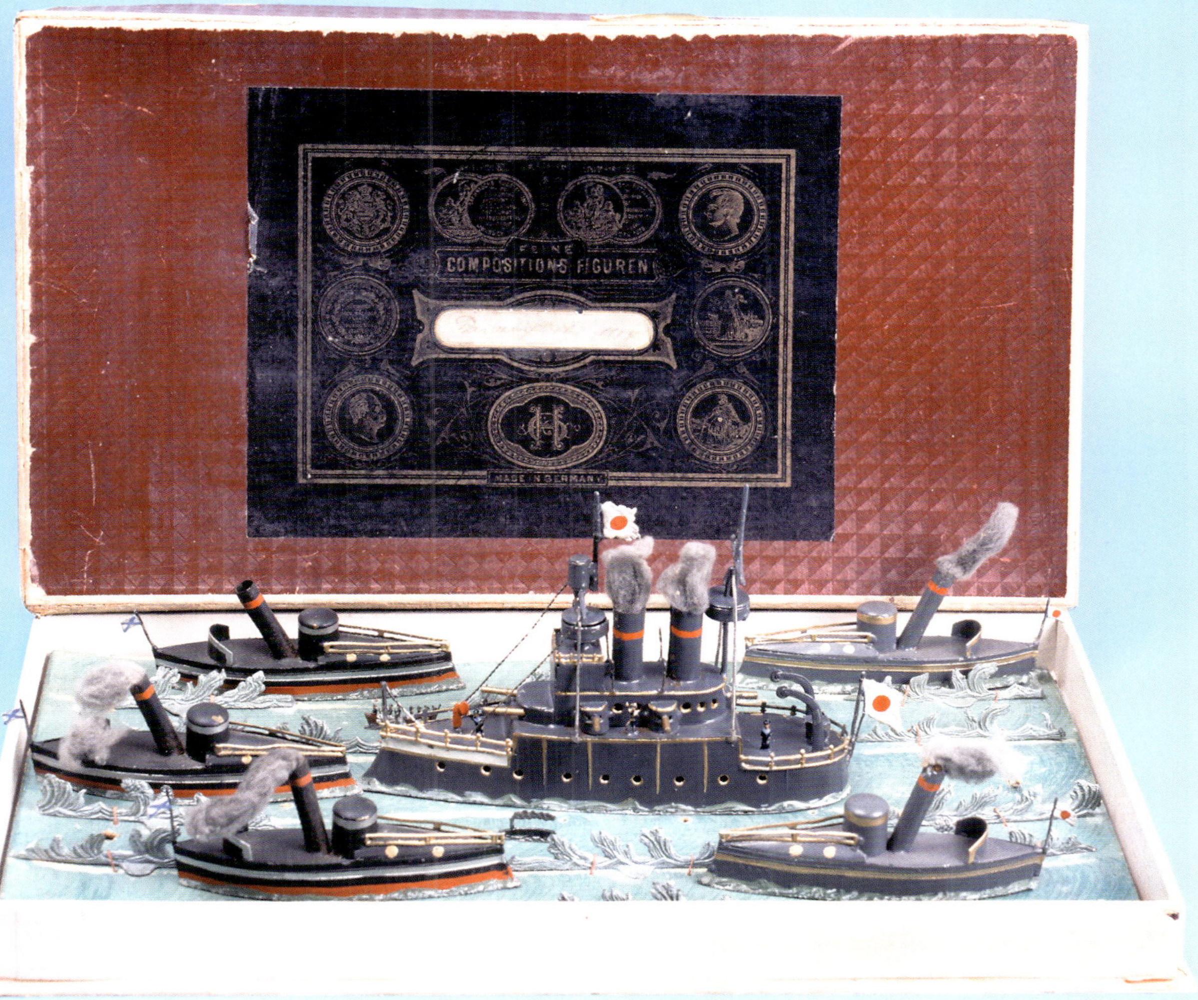

HN-2 HN-1 HN-3

Horndlein

From the 1930's, all 9″ long.
Left to right:
(HN-2), (HN-1), (HN-3).

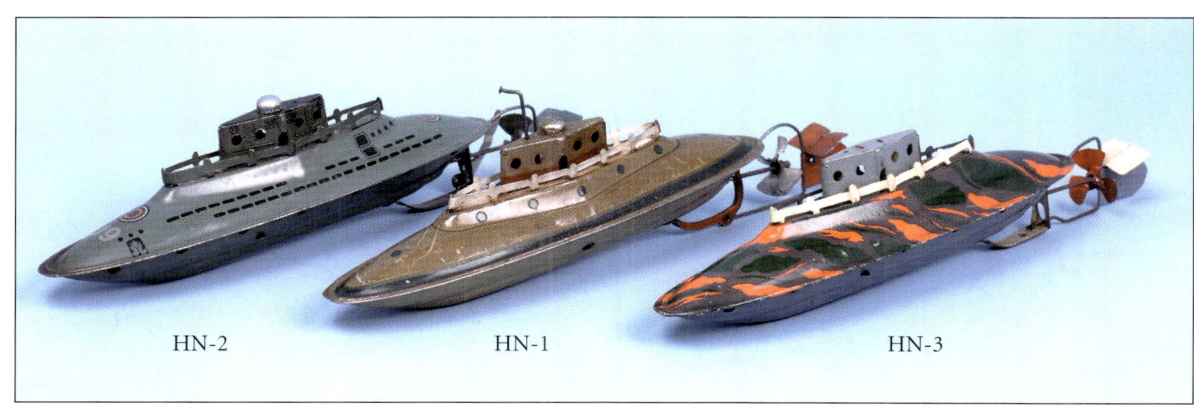

(IR-4) 6″. Made in the late 19th or early 20th century, this whimsical boat carries a bisque figure and its mechanism causes it to tack back and forth while sailing across the floor.

(IR-5) 6″.
Great litho on this early 20th century clockwork battleship. This could possibly be made by Gunthermann.

132

IR-4

IR-5

1926. Rear: (CK-6), 9″ #168.
Front: (CK-8) 4″ #173.
Nonpowered floor toys.

1926-30. Left to right: (CK-12) 10″ #237,
(CK-11) 9″ #226/7, (CK-2) 9″ #226.
A very popular clockwork floor toy,
which was copied by other manufacturers.

1938-58: Left to right:
(CK-4) 13″ #351,
(CK-1) 13″ #354.
Utilizing the same hull, these realistically
designed ships are reminiscent of the German
pocket battleship *Admiral Graff Spee* and
the liners *Bremen* and *Europa*.

1926. Rear: (CK-5) 9″ #289.
Front, left to right: (CK-10) 9″, (CK-7) 9″ #287N.
Clockwork water toys based upon the same hull.

These clockwork wooden boats were made in Germany during the 1920's and sold by FAO Schwarz in 1927. By 1937-38, they could be found in the Tri-ang catalog. Top to bottom: (KLR-2) 31″, (KLR-1) 25″, (KLR-3) 18″.

Georg Levy (GELY)

1920's. Back: (LG-1) 13″ #152. Front, left to right: (LG-3) 10″ #29, (LG-4) 9″ #109, (LG-2) 7″ #108 All are clockwork floor toys.

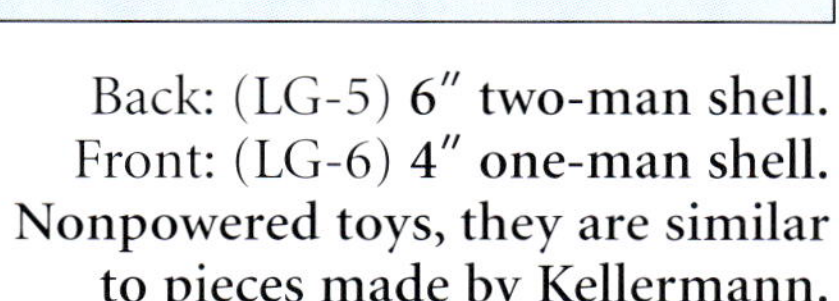

Back: (LG-5) 6″ two-man shell. Front: (LG-6) 4″ one-man shell. Nonpowered toys, they are similar to pieces made by Kellermann.

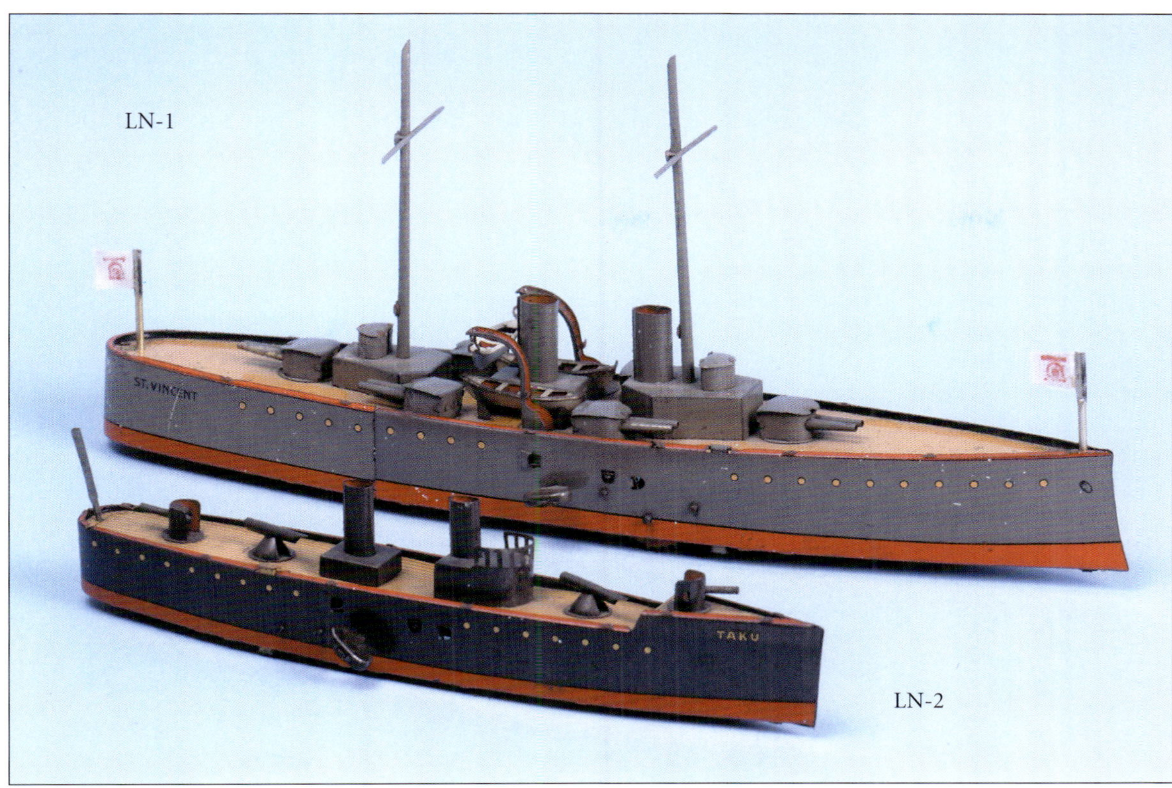

Spring driven floor toys.
Back: (LN-1) 1914-38, 13″ #672 *St. Vincent*. Between 1917-37 this was also issued as #729, *Emden*. In front is (LN-2) 9″ #671 *Taku*, sold between 1913 and 1935. It was also made as #728 *U-2* between 1914 and 1918. Although it looks nothing like a submarine, #728 was named to take advantage of the great notoriety of U-boats during WW I. The actual *Taku* was a torpedo boat built 1898 in Germany as the *Hai-Ching* for the Chinese Navy. In June 1900 it was captured by the British, became a German war reparation, and was renamed *Taku*. Based in Tsingtao, it was scuttled at the outbreak of WW I. The *Emden* requires an entire book for its tale.

Between 1955 and 1981, Lehmann produced the 900 series of plastic clockwork ships.
Back: (LN-3) 7″ #906 *Mars*.
Middle row, left to right:
(LN-4) 7″ #904 *Columbus*,
(LN-5) 7″ #905 *Unus*,
(LN-6) 7″ #907 *Tina*.
Front row, left to right:
(LN-8) 7″ #904 *Columbus*,
(LN-7) 7″ #908 *Fortuna*.
At first the ships were boxed, later on they came blister packed.

Back: (M-42) **1909-15, 46″ #5050/11D**, *Kaiserin Augusta Victoria*.
Front: (M- 45) **1915-25, 8″ #5026/20**, *Augusta Victoria*.
On its maiden voyage, May 10, 1906, the *Kaiserin Auguste Victoria*
(note the spelling difference) was the largest ocean liner in the world. The 5050/11
is usually found with three or four stacks; this version, however, accurately represents
her namesake with only two. She is also properly flying the Hamburg-America Line's
company colors on the aft mast. While this ship is powered by a large two-cylinder
reversing steam engine, it was also offered with an electric motor.
Interestingly, the #5050/11D is never accurately depicted in Märklin catalogs except
on the "Schiffe" section frontispiece. Below are Märklin's largest and smallest liners.
The #5050/11D weighs an incredible 30 pounds, certainly no toy for a small boy!

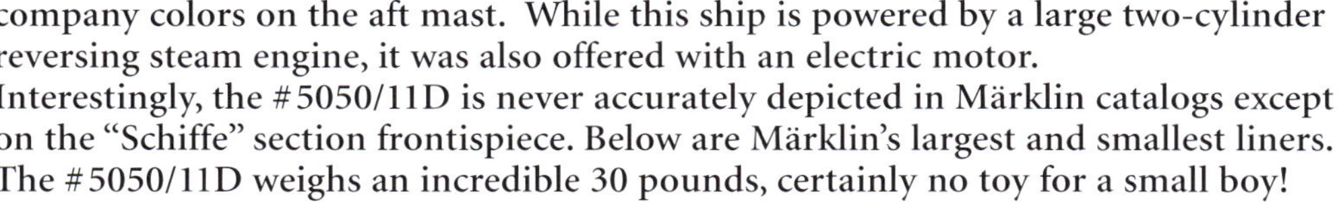
M-42

M-45

Apparently this toy was designed for three stacks when it was discovered that the real *Kaiserin Auguste Victoria* was a two-stacker! (Note the stack-less base just behind the flying bridge.) The wonderful condition of this boat after almost one hundred years is evidenced by the original life preserver ring hanging on the rail opposite the pilot house

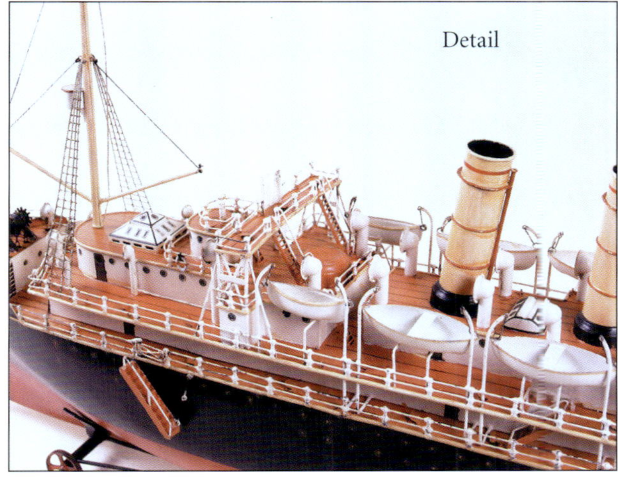

Detail

Detail

1909 Catalog. The only accurate picture of #5050/11. The interior catalog cut erroneously shows an enlarged #5050/9. Shown here as the Norddeutcher Lloyd Blue Riband holder *Kaiser Wilhelm der Grosse*, this version correctly has 4 stacks.

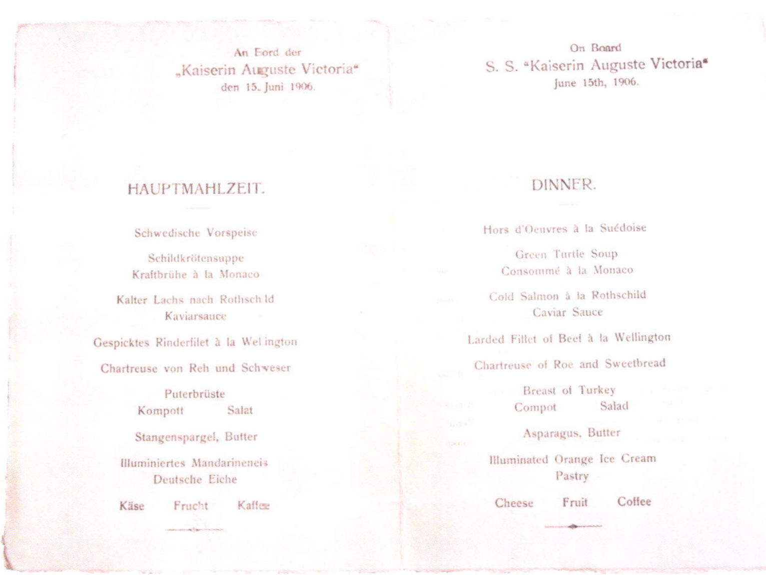

(M-21) 1909-15, 38″ #5050/9D, *Kronprinz Wilhelm*
This vessel flies the Norddeutscher Lloyd company flag from the aft mast as would her "schnelldampfer" namesake. The ship is the second size of the 5050 series, weighing in at 22 pounds. While available in clockwork and electric versions, like her larger 46″ sister, it has a two-cylinder reversing steam plant.
On her maiden voyage in 1901 the ship captured the Blue Riband. After serving as a commerce raider in 1915, she was forced by needed repairs to put into the then neutral port of Newport News, Va. Seized by the US Government in 1917, she was renamed *Von Steuben* for use as a Navy transport. The ship appears on the 10 cent parcel post stamp of 1912.

138

M-21

(M -37) 1909-15, 28″
#5050 E/7, *Deutschland*
Smallest of the 5050
(largest) series, this
ship was offered
powered by clockwork,
steam or electric.
This is the electric
version as shown by
the searchlight on the
foremast. Most often
5050/E7 is found
as *Carmania* with
appropriately painted
red Cunard Line stacks.
The liner *Deutschland*
was a four stacker.
It was HAPAG's only
Blue Ribband Holder.

Hamburg America vs.
Nordeutscher Lloyd.

Detail

Crew members busy themselves at the
stern of *Deutschland*. The flag at the stern
always indicates the ship's country of
origin, in this case pre WW I Germany.
On the 5050 series names often appeared
on the stern as well as the bow.

(M-55)
1915-1921, 19″ #5044/49 *Amerika*.
While this ship is clockwork
powered, it was the smallest
liner to be available with a full
reciprocating steam engine.
The Swiss flag is simply another
one of those toy maker anomalies.

M-55

Left to right:
(M-47) 18″ #5026 M/47,
Augusta Victoria,
(M-36) 10″ #5026 M/26
Lausanne,
(M-46) 9″ #5026 M/23
George Washington.
Between 1915 and 1927 the
"put-put" or "mysteriosbetrieb"
version was available in
the 5026 series.

M-47

M-36

M-46

Clockwise from center rear:
(M-13) 18″ #5026/47 *Le Touriste,* (M-27) 14″ #5026/37, *Geneve,*
(M-46) 9″ #5026 M/23, *George Washington,* (M-36) 10″ #5026 M/26, *Lausanne,*
(M-45) 8″ #5026/20, *Augusta Victoria,* (M-29) 11″ #5026/29, *Luzern,*
(M-24) 13″ #5026/33, *Deutchland,* (M-12) 16″ #5026/42, *Amerika.*
Between 1915 and 1927 the 5026 series consisted of as many as eight sizes.
Most came with names on their bows. Most also used the Norddeutscher Lloyd
company flag, although it was not necessarily the line of the actual ship.

(M-22) **1915, 26″ #5045/68.** The intermediate size liner *Rhein.* This ship is clockwork driven. It was also available with a single-cylinder steam plant.

(M-14) **1919-31, 28″ #5050/7, 2nd Series,** *Resolute.*
Sun-bleached, this toy was rescued from a travel agent's window. While retaining its clockwork motor, it was modified for display by punched-through portholes on the port side (since restored) for illumination. Oddly, the ship has only one anchor and chain port. It has the late version Märklin trademark on the rudder. A HAPAG liner (note company flag on aft mast) would have proudly displayed a banded black-over-white-over-red paint scheme on its three stacks. Norddeutscher Lloyd, their competition, used buff colored stacks. Between 1928 and 1935 *Resolute* was employed solely in cruise service.

(M-58) 1919-1931, 38″ #5050/9 (2nd Series), *Rhein.*
By 1921 this later, more modern 5050 series had replaced that of 1909, yet the earlier 5050/7 & 5050/9 were still pictured in the 1923 English catalog! The largest 2nd Series liner, the 46″ #5050/11, was illustrated in Märklin's 1929 catalog, but by then only 28″ and 38″ ships were available.

M-58

143

(M-30) 1919-1931, 38″ #5050/9 (2nd Series), *Columbus.*
Quite a few of these display models used by travel agencies still exist. This version differs from the toy in that it has only two stacks, no mechanism, lamps inside which shine through portholes punched in the side, and a special stand. The flag on the jack staff indicates that she still has her Weser River pilot on board and the foremast flag shows she is outbound from Bremerhaven for America. In December 1939 while attempting a return to Germany, the *Columbus* was intercepted by the destroyer *HMS Hyperion* 320 miles east of Cape Hatteras. The crew set the ship on fire and scuttled it.

M-30

Left to right:
(M-50) 16″ #5062/40,
(M-52) 11″ #5062/29,
(M-41) 9″ #5062/23.
The last hurrah for Märklin liners, this series between 1927 and 1934 is all that was left of a once great fleet. All boats are clockwork powered.

(M-16) 1915-1929, 30″ #5066/75 *Loreley,*
(M-18) 1921-1929, 18″ #5066/46.
While certainly more to a realistic scale, these two lack the whimsical qualities of their paddle-wheeler predecessors.

(M-59) 1902, 41″ #1096, first series clockwork battleship *Iowa*.
This early version has lifeboats with insertable masts and sails.
At the time this was Märklin's largest ship, however, in 1904 it was
listed as being 115cm (45″). The *USS Iowa BB-4* cost one million
dollars by the time it was finished in 1896. It was famous for having
fired the first shot under the command of Capt. Sampson
(later Admiral) at the battle of Santiago.

M-59

(M-49) 1912-1915, 34″
#5130 D/8, *Baltimore.*
This steam powered version is commonly referred to as a 2nd series battleship. It is distinguished by its rounded protruding bow in contrast to the flat-sided ram bow of the 1st series.

Left: (M-11) 1909-1912, 21″
#5105, *Meteor.*
Right: (M-32) 1909-1912, 16″
#5103, *New York.*
Both of these clockwork "Panzerkreuzers" were also available with steam engines.

(M-25) 1911-34, 16″ #5079/42, *Whipple.*
This series of torpedo boat came in four sizes.
The real *Whipple* (DD-15) was in the Torpedo Boat
Destroyer Division that from 1907 to 1909 accompanied
"The Great White Fleet" around the world.

M-25

(M-23) 1909-1915, 15″ #5106/38, *H.M.S. Alexandra.*
A transitional design, this clockwork gunboat
came with a photo of its original owner.

M-23

M-44

Postcard marked "John Wilcox 1909."

(M-44) 1904-9, 20″ #1080/2 or #5080/50, *S 57.*
This is the early version with the
green and black paint scheme.

Gebrüder Märklin

(M-35) 1915, 36″ #5128 D/9, *Maryland.*
In their 1915 catalog, Märklin lists three deck configurations for their 90cm *Linienschiff:* German, English and French. This steam driven French version was obviously not sent to, nor named to suit, the market for which it was designed.

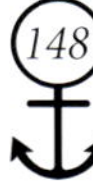

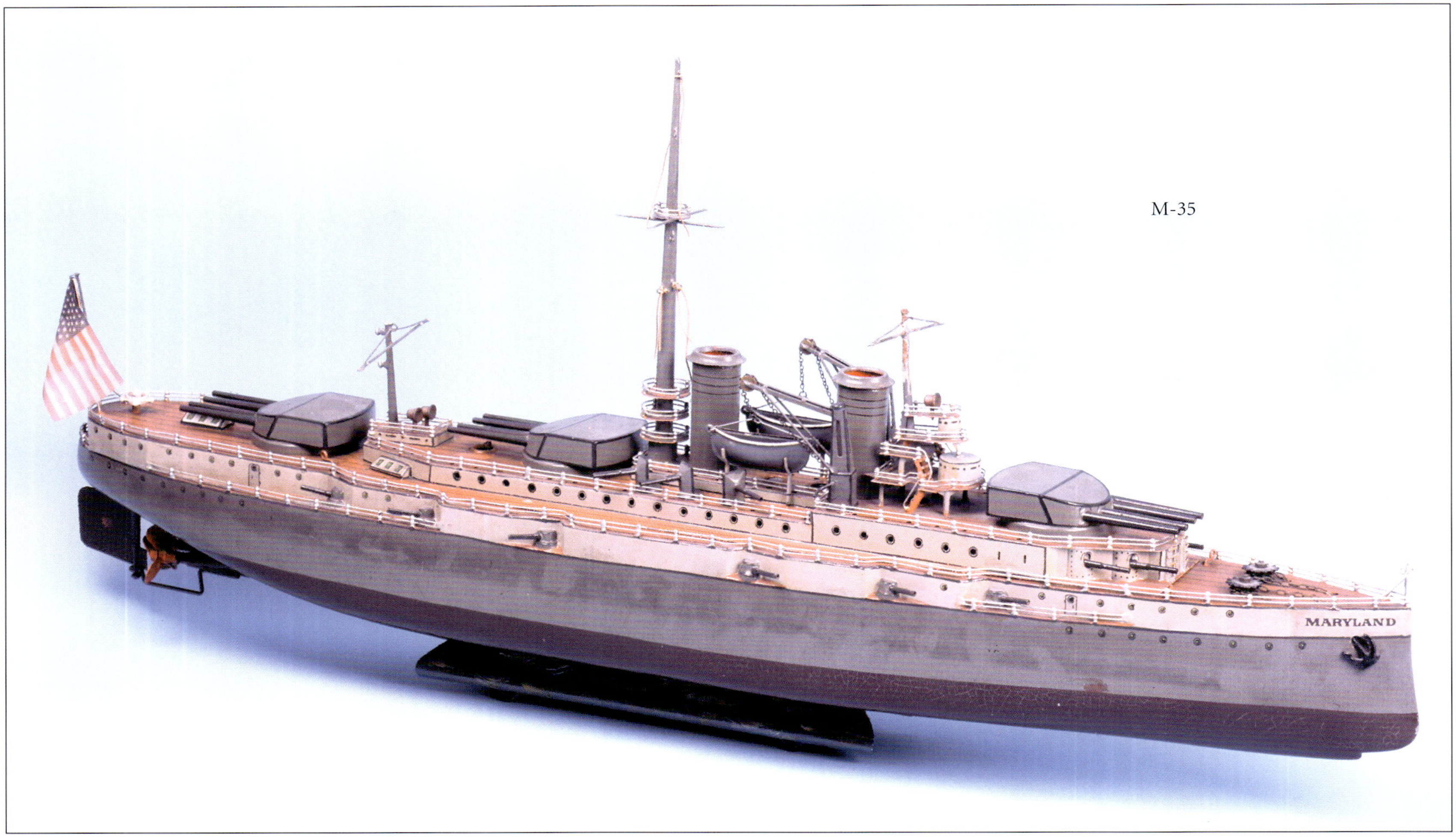

M-35

Rear: (M-1) 1915-34, 36″, #5129/9.
Front: (M-51) 1915-28, 9″ #5107 M/23, *Wilmington*.
The third series battleships were much more realistic, this one having a
typical German dreadnought configuration of WW I. This particular ship
is clockwork powered, but was available with a two-cylinder steam engine.
Little "put-put" *Wilmington* was designed for the bathtub.

Left to right: (M-3) **1915-34, 27″ #5129/7;** (M-2) **1915-21, 21″ #5129/52;** (M-60) **1915-34, 18″ #5129/47.** In 1915 there were seven sizes in the 5129 series, from 13″ to 90″. By 1934, their last year, five remained. These three are clockwork powered.

Left: (M-28) **1915-1928, 13″ #5107 M/29** *Helena.*
Right: (M-4) **1915-1934, 13″ #5129/33** *Lavoisier.*
Helena is "Mysteriosbetrieb" while *Lavoisier,*
the smallest of the 5129 series, is clockwork powered.

Left: (M-5) **1915-1921, 16″ #5129/42,** *Schwalbe.*
Right: (M-17) **1915-1934, 15″ #5129/37** with
late style paint scheme.

5110/33

5110/40

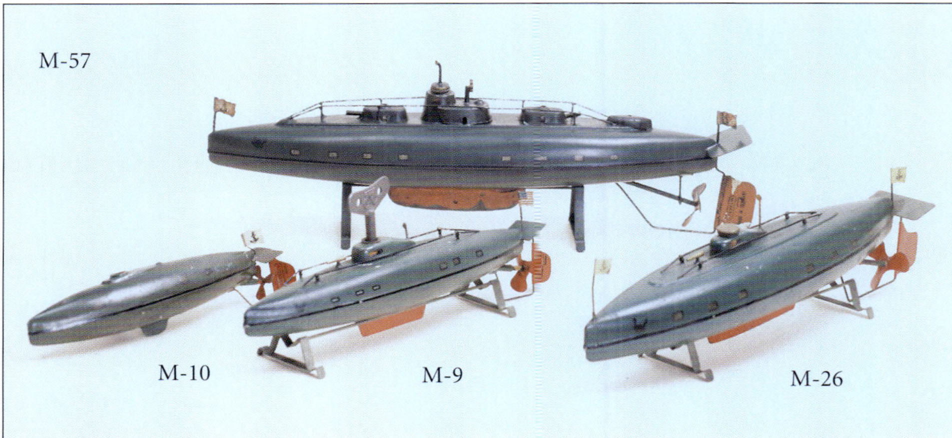

(M-56) 1914-18, 22″, "Unterseeboot" *U-9*. It is unusual to find a named, or numbered, Märklin submarine. This one, however, is apparently trading on the fame of Lt. Otto Weddigen, who, in September 1914 commanding the *U-9*, sank three British armored cruisers within a matter of minutes. For this action he was awarded Germany's highest honor, the medal "Pour le Merite."

M-20

M-19

M-6

M-31

M-8

Gebrüder Märklin

Rear: (M-20) 30″ #5081/76.
Middle row, left to right:
(M-19) 22″ #5081/57,
(M-6) 16″ #5081/41,
(M-8) 8″ #5108/29.
Front: (M-31) 9″ #5108/23.
The 5081 series had movable dive planes geared to the clockwork motor, which alternately dove and surfaced the boat. They were cataloged from 1915 until 1938. The smaller 5108 series had fixed bow and stern planes, relying solely on progress through the water to submerge. The 5110 series replaced them in the early 1930's. In 1927 F.A.O. Schwarz sold the 30″ sub for the then princely sum of $25.

M-57

M-10

M-9

M-26

Rear: (M-57) 15 1/2″ #5110/40.
Front, left to right:
(M-10) 8″ #5110/19,
(M-9) 10″ #5110/26,
(M-26) 12″ #5110/33.
This series (4 sizes) was cataloged from 1931 to 1939. The tail fin was the means used for submerging the boat. By 1939 submarines were the only boats cataloged by Märklin. Today it is quite a find to come across an operable sub, due to the rust caused by accumulated interior water.

(M-43) **1900-1902, 31″ #1075** *Chicago.*
Märklin's largest paddle-wheeler. Catalog shows only
#1076 propeller driven version *Hohenzollern,* which
by 1904 was the only version made.

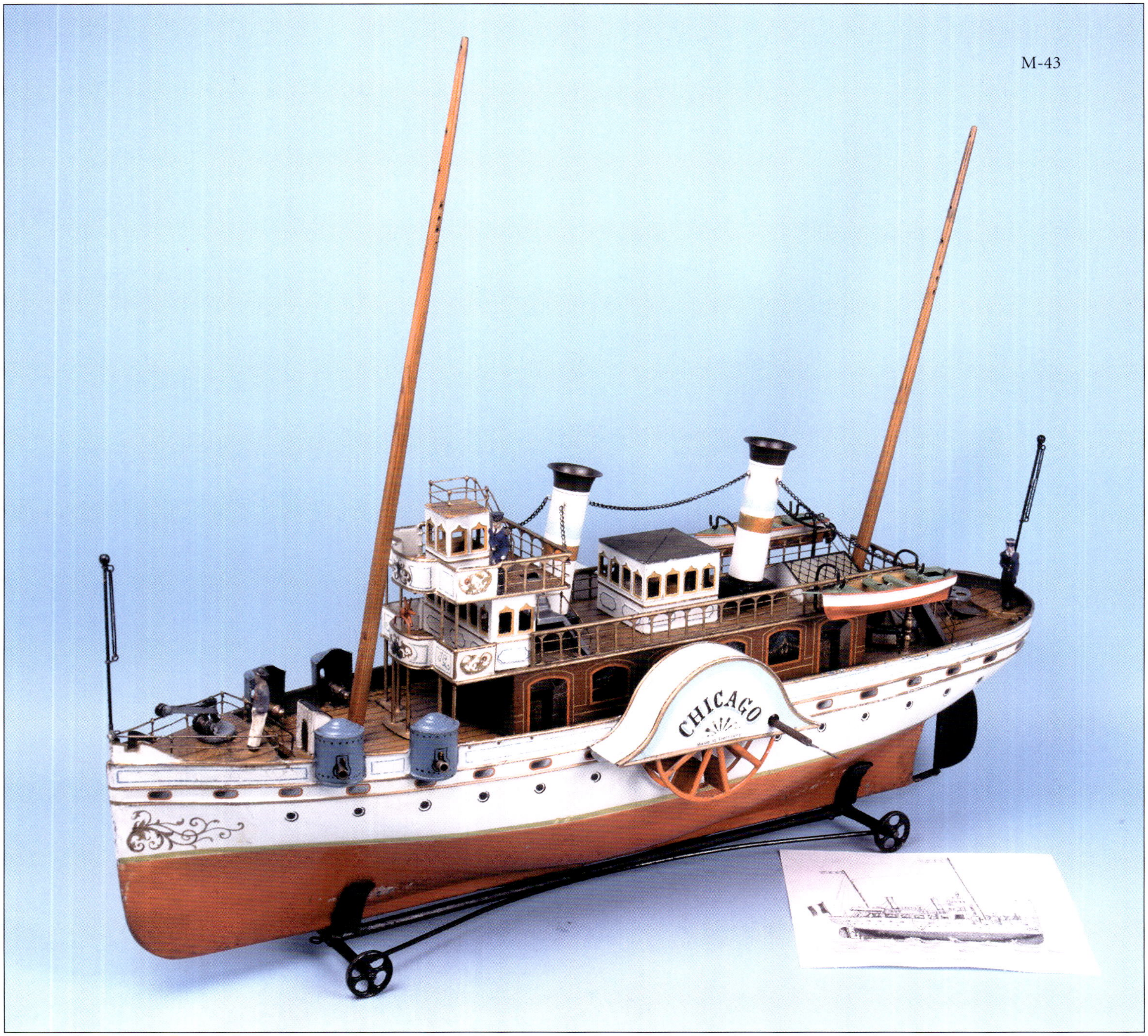

M-43

CHICAGO

152

Chicago bridge with original captain.
These composition figures, which could be purchased separately, have wire spikes in their bases that insert into small tube-lined holes in the deck. One protrudes below the bridge on the left.

Close-up photos show the marvelous attention to detail. Note the perspective painted into the cabin windows. Märklin used the same wheel for the steering mechanism as for the ship-stand. The metal pressings used for the bridge and upper deck cabins can be found in early rail cars.

Sailor tends the anchor crane on *Chicago's* foredeck.

(M-53) 1909-12, 13″ #5040/34, *Blenheim*,
(M-33) 1909-12, 9″ #5040/22, *St. Paul*.
This clockwork driven series came in four sizes, 9″ to 17″.
The largest size was also available with a steam engine.

(M-48) 1907-09, 12″ #5056/30, *Tip-Top*.
This motor yacht came in four sizes, the three largest of which
were cataloged as being available with an electric motor.
Tip-Top, however, is the smallest size, yet electrically powered!

154

M-15

M-39

(M-15) **1909-28, 24″**
#5064/62, *Yolanda,*
(M-39) **1915-28, 16″**
#5064/41, *Yolanda.*
The 24″ yacht *Yolanda*
was one of Märklin's longest
cataloged and most popular
ships. It was available only
with a clockwork motor.

155

M-34

M-38

M-54

Left to right: (M-34)
1925-34, 11″ #5061/29M;
(M-38)
1915-34, 9″ #5100 M/24;
(M-54)
1915-34, 4″ #5100 M/12.
All of these motor jolly-boats
are "Mysteriosbetrieb."
5061/29 was also available
with a clockwork motor.
The other two came only
with the "put-put"
steam plant.

Back row, left to right:
(MR-1) 4″,
(MR-5) 4″.
Middle row, left to right:
(MR-7) 4″,
(MR-6) 4″,
(MR-4) 4″.
Front, left to right:
(MR-3) 3″,
(MR-2) 3″.

1920-30.
Left to right:
(MK-3) 14″ *Vulkan,*
(MK-4) 12″ *Mars*
marked WK,
(MK-2) 9″ *Mars,*
(MK-1) 9″ *Mars.*
The same spring driven
toys were made under
the Wilhelm Krauss and
Mohr & Krauss labels.

Oro-Werke (Orobr)

Left: (O-2) **8″, Orobr #120.**
Right: (RC-2) **8″, Reil #320.**

(O-4) **12″.**
Shown below is a 1930's spring motor driven floor toy liner with battery power to illuminate the port and starboard running lights.

Back: (O-5) **9″, #134.**
Left middle: (O-3) **11″.**
Right middle: (O-1) **11″.**
Front: (O-2) **8″, #120.**
Note the non-litho stacks which seem to be one of the primary departures from Reil production.

Top: (EP-3) **1902, 11″ #128/3.**
Bottom: (EP-4) **9″ #128/2.**
These steam powered ships are each driven by a turbine wheel attached to their respective propeller shafts. It is difficult to believe that the paint on the larger boat was once as lustrous as that of the smaller.

(EP-10) **10″.** Although this clockwork a[...] boat is not trademarked, it displays ma[...] Plank characteristics. The outriggers fo[...] upward to conserve space in its box.

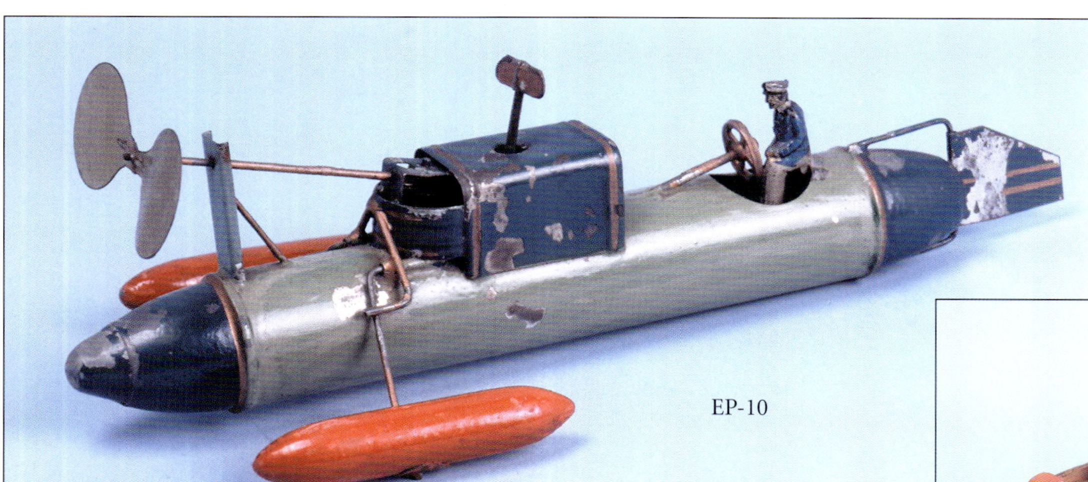

Left to right: (EP-5) & (EP-6) **1902, 10″ #128B.**
Possibly produced at different times, these variants of the same steam toy have been faithfully restored to their original paint schemes.

(EP-1) 15″. New in 1903, this "torpedo boat with strong clockwork motor" was cataloged in four sizes ranging from 8″ to 19″. Its mechanism is wound by rotating the torpedo tube.

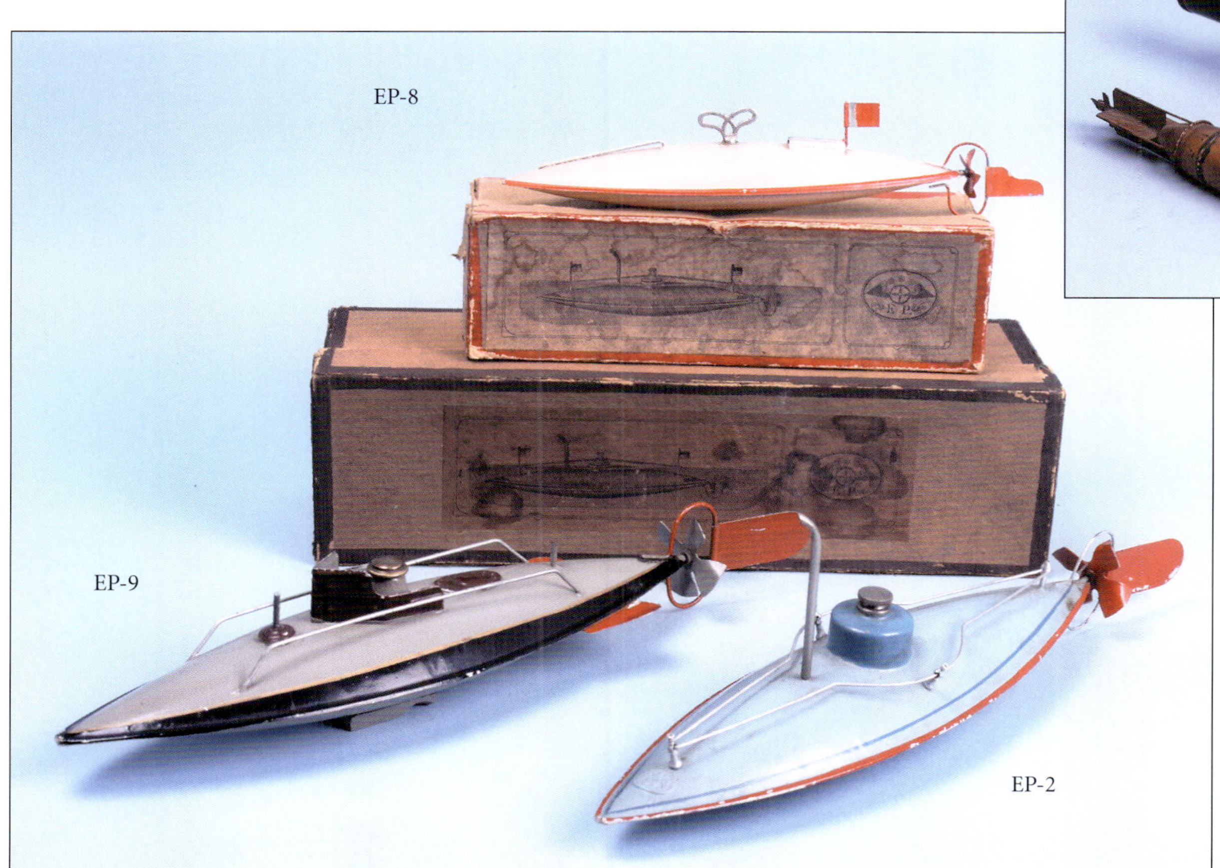

(EP-7) 8″.
A spring mechanism ejects the torpedo from its tube. The torpedo is not powered.

Top: (EP-8) 8″ #460/1.
Front, left to right:
(EP-9) 12″, (EP-2) 12″ #460/3. Introduced in 1903 under the banner, "a new operating toy for the mature child," these clockwork diving submarines were made until WW I. The boat in the left foreground has no trademark, but there is little doubt as to its origin.

Reil & Co.

1900-08, spring driven floor toys.
Clockwise from the left rear: (RC-1) 11″ #207 liner
(note trademark at the lower right corner of the box label),
(RC-3) 11″ cruiser which was shown in the 1902 Sears catalog,
(RC-2) 8″ #320 paddle-wheeler (see Orobr section for comparison),
(RC-4) 9″ #108 torpedo boat. All boats have litho stacks.

RR-5   T-79   T-25

Richter

Early 1900's Richter spring driven toys.
Left to right:
(RR-5) ship, 8″,
(T-79) horse car, 12″,
(T-25) trolley, 6″.
All these toys share features such as wheels, railings, etc.

RR-5

(RR-5) 1900, 8″ spring wound riverboat floor toy. This ship has many of the details in common with other Richter toys, such as wheels, railings and lithography.

161

(RG-3) 1875, 28″ w/o bowsprit, steam powered *Furst Bismarck*. This impressive toy was found in South America covered with a coat of flat white paint. It has been lovingly restored to its original grandeur.

The stern of *Furst Bismarck* shows its elaborate steering mechanism as well as the rudder which is hollow and fabricated from brass. The ship also retains its original boat stand.

RG-3

(RG-1) 1875, 21″ w/o bowsprit, #2111 steam powered *Kaiser Wilhelm.*
Until recently this ship was believed to have been produced by Lutz.
The discovery of an 1875 catalog has proven otherwise.

RG-1

RG-4

RG-2

UK-84

(UK-84) 1880's, 9″ clockwork paddle-wheeler.
While not positively identified, the boat is
definitely German and possibly Rock & Graner.
It might, however, be a bit crudely made for
their work.

Rear: (RG-4) 1875, 19″ #1398 Thames River Boat #1, *Rhein.*
Front: (RG-2) 1875, 15″ #1399 steamship #2, *Ocean.*
Both boats are clockwork but were available nonpowered. There is a striking
similarity between the *Rhein* and the paddle-wheeler appearing in *The George
Brown Sketchbook,* leading to the probability that Brown's boat was an import.

Karl Rosenbauer (KRN)

1920-30, left to right:
(KRN-1) **18″**,
(KRN-3) **12″**,
(KRN-2) **7″**.
Very little is known about
this manufacturer.

SR-4

(SR-4) 1900, 31″ #828/2 steam powered *Kurfurst Friedrich Wilhelm.* The metalwork of this rare dreadnought is quite crude, typical of Schoenner's work. The ship was available in two sizes and in a clockwork version.

UK-46

(UK-46) 8″. Early 20th century speedboat. Schoenner anyone?

In 1900 these steam powered saloon screw steamers came in 5 sizes. Shown are the two smallest. Left to right: (SR-3) 15″ #811 and (SR-1) 12″ #810.

SR-3

SR-1

Left to right: (C-8) 13″ and (C-14) 15″ river boats could have been made for Carette. They display many typically Schoenner characteristics. The boat on the right (SR-2) 1882, 10″ *Angostura* is marked J.S.

(UK-89) 14″. Even the original box is of little help in the positive identification of this possibly Schoenner product.

(SR-5) 1905, 8″.
This small clockwork boat has been completely restored. When it was found it had been stripped of paint and totally dissembled. Identification was possible due to Claude Jeanmaire's book, *Toys of Nuremburg, Jean Schoenner's Toy Railways and Ships*. The toy is shown for sale at $2.15 per dozen in the 1905 Butler Brothers catalog.

From the 1950's through the 70's Schuco made a number of plastic boats, some of which are shown here.
Back:
(SO-4) 1971, 21″ #763 380 *Fontainebleau.*
Front, left to right:
(SO-2) 1954, 6″ #3004 speedboat;
(SO-3) 1953, 9″ #5411 *Navico* speedboat;
(SO-1) 1963-75, 12″ #5552 submarine.
Although some clockwork boats were offered, all these are battery powered.

(SH-1) Set of early 20th century flats contemporary with Heyde. These figures are like those used with Märklin ships.

SH-1

Left to right:
(ST-21) 16″, (ST-6) 11″ #3500/3,
(ST-3) 9″ #3500/2, (ST-12) 7″ #3500/1.
Shown here is a series of clockwork
liners that has all the obvious Staudt
characteristics. They were made
between 1907 and 1930.

In 1912 Staudt cataloged
6 sizes of "American" tugboats.
Back: (ST-2) 10″ #3314.
Front: (ST-16) 8″ #3312.

By 1928 Staudt had become a
division of Fleischmann. The 3612
series of clockwork "Salondampfers"
are shown in the 1930 price list.
At the rear: (ST-5) 17″ #3612/6
(was listed in the 1928
Moko catalog as #5465/6).
Middle: (ST-17) 16″ #3612/5.
Front row, left to right:
(ST-4) 11″ #3612/3,
(ST-15) 9″ #3612/2,
(ST-18) 7″ #3612/1,
(ST-19) 4″.
All boats were in production
since before WW I.

ST-13
ST-8
ST-20
ST-7

In 1912 these shovel-nosed warships appeared as the 3317 series.
Left to right:
(ST-13) 19″ #3317/4,
(ST-20) 14″ #3317/3,
(ST-7) 16″ #3317/3,
(ST-8) 10″ #3317/2.
All are clockwork powered and have distinctively shaped rudders.

Left: (ST-14) 21″. This warship was purchased at auction and professionally restored using (ST-1) as a guide.
Right: (ST-1) 1907-12, 14″ #3200/4. The toy came with its original box, marked only with a distributor's label.

ST-14
ST-1

ST-10
ST-11

Top: (ST-10) 1912, 8″ #3199.
Bottom: (ST-11) 1912, 9″ #3200.
Note once more the uniquely shaped rudders.
The smoke shaped key also is distinctively Staudt.

169

(ST-9) 8″ #3239. One of five sizes of this motorboat design listed by Staudt between 1907 and 1930. Few other toy makers made the same item for so long a period.

ST-9

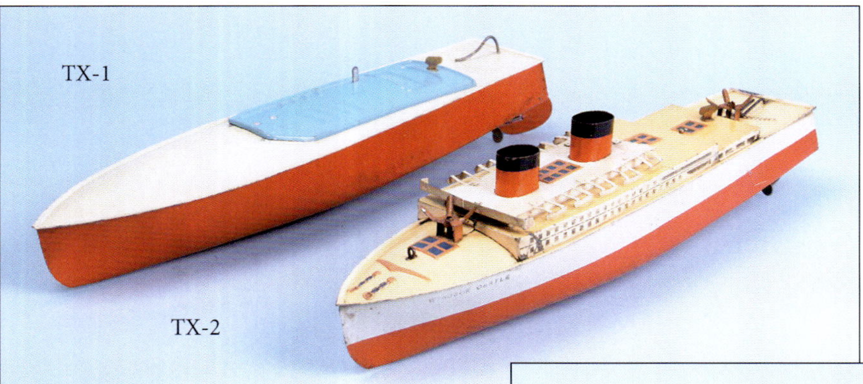

TX-1

TX-2

Trix

Left to right:
(TX-1) 1937-38, 17″ #2006 electric powered speedboat;
(TX-2) 17″ #2005 clockwork powered liner. Both boats came equipped with either clockwork or electric motors which were interchangeable.

TX-1

(U-9) Great graphics and a title for every market. The warships are nonpowered and range in size from 3″ to 4″ in length. This set is shown in the 1902-6 Gammage catalog.

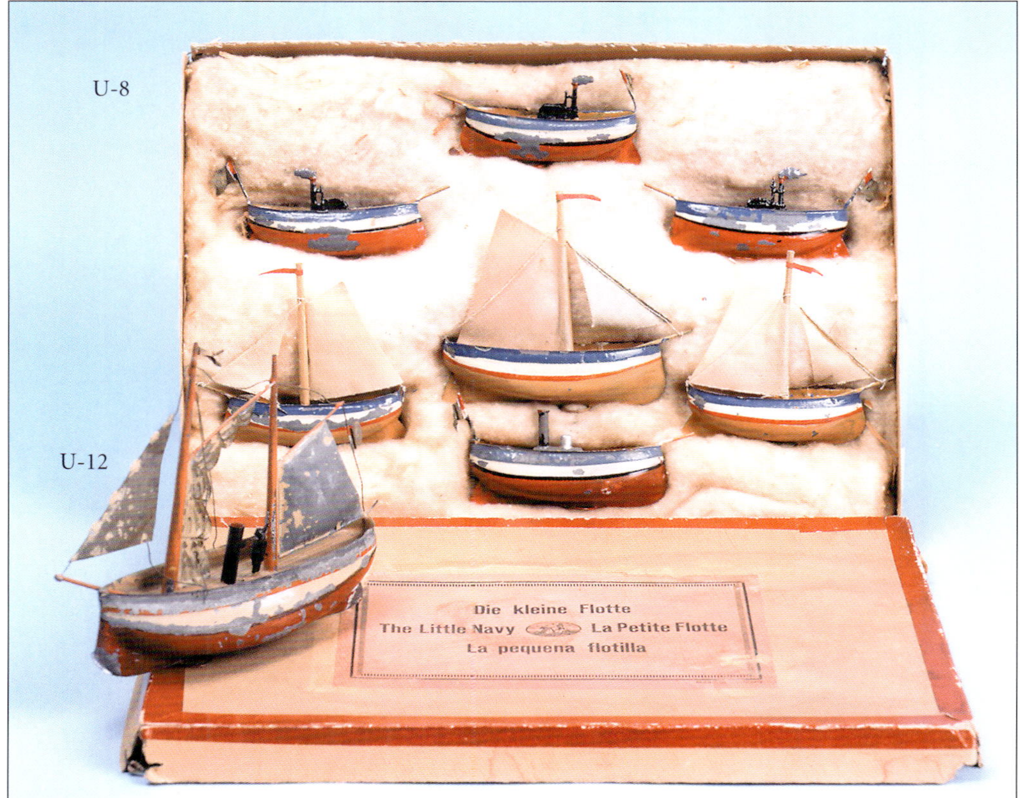

U-9

U-8

U-12

(U-8) Even when kept carefully for close to 100 years in their box, these little beauties have shed some paint. They are clones of Fleischmann products of the same vintage. The steam/sail boat (U-12) sitting on the lid, and not part of the set, is all of 5″ long. All boats are nonpowered.

These clockwork riverboats are shown in the 1900 Ullmann & Engelmann catalog. From top to bottom: (U-1) 12″, (U-3) 12″ U&E #04734/1, (U-4) 10″, (U-10) 8″, (U-6) 8″ U&E #04732. By the 1920's they were being produced under the Fleischmann name.

Family group figures were used by several manufacturers including Bing, Staudt and Fleischmann. Sometimes held in place by a clip, and more often than not missing, these on the Uebelacker boat are not detachable.

172

U-1

U-3

U-4

U-10

U-6

U-11

(U-11) 1900's, 10″, 4″ and 3″. This set of ships was cataloged in the 1920's by Falk. It is shown as #2014 along with warships and a sub produced by Arnold. Another case of widespread German toy maker inter-relationships.

U-2

(U-2) 1905, 8″.
The trademark at the bow differentiates this charming rower from that found in the 1905 Carette catalog. It is shown there as #738/1 with a dog perched at the stern. A larger version with a passenger was also available.

173

U-5

(U-5)
1900, 24″ U&E #04735/60. Shown here is the largest cataloged Uebelacher boat. It is also shown in early Fleischmann catalogs. The brass trademark plate at the stern above the winding crank makes positive identification.

GZ-1

(GZ-1). A scene by an unknown (trademark GZ or ZG) German maker depicting what seems to be the siege of Port Arthur during the Russo-Japanese War of 1904-5.

Top: (UK-1). Bottom: (UK-4).
These two wooden sets are identical except for their boxes. Although the specific manufacturer is unknown, it is safe to conclude that they are German.

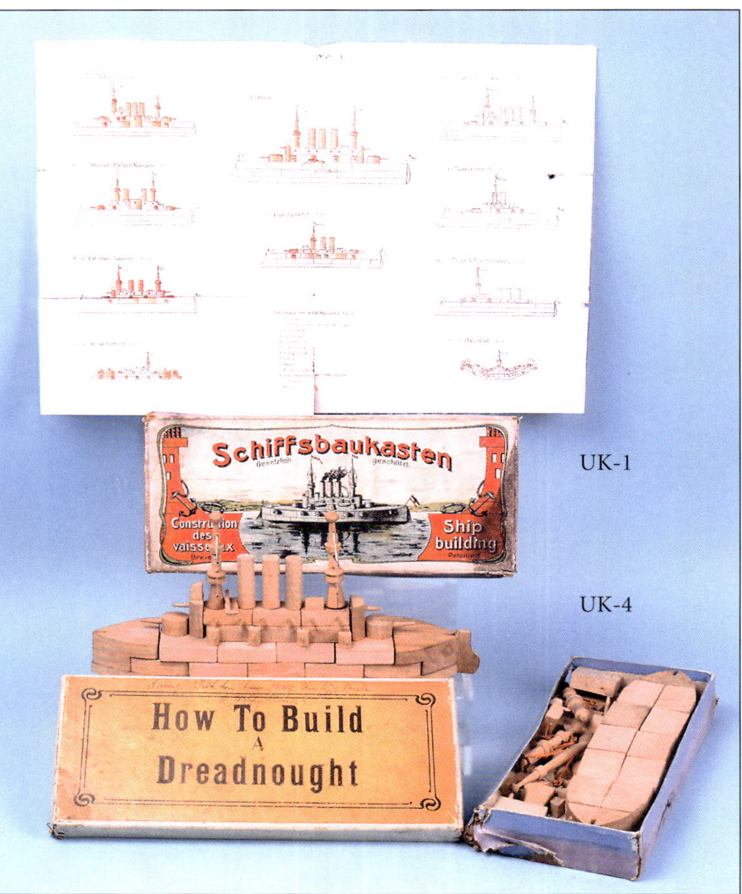

UK-1

UK-4

UK-24

UK-24) 10″.
The trademark of an intertwined JS is not much help in identifying this 19th century German boat building set. The hull is tin as are the paddle-wheel boxes and stack.

(UK-22) **6″.**
German clockwork toy that rocks when wound. See *Les Bateaux Jouet* **(P. 76).**

UK-22

UK-51

Unknown

(UK-51) **19″. Although very similar to a Bing rower, this clockwork oarsman has a paddle-wheel-like action rather than the more natural rowing movement.**

UK-45

(UK-45) **19″. This early 1900's clockwork battleship is rather crude in its construction, but wonderfully symmetrical in design. Its manufacturer is another one of those toy mysteries.**

Italian Manufacturers

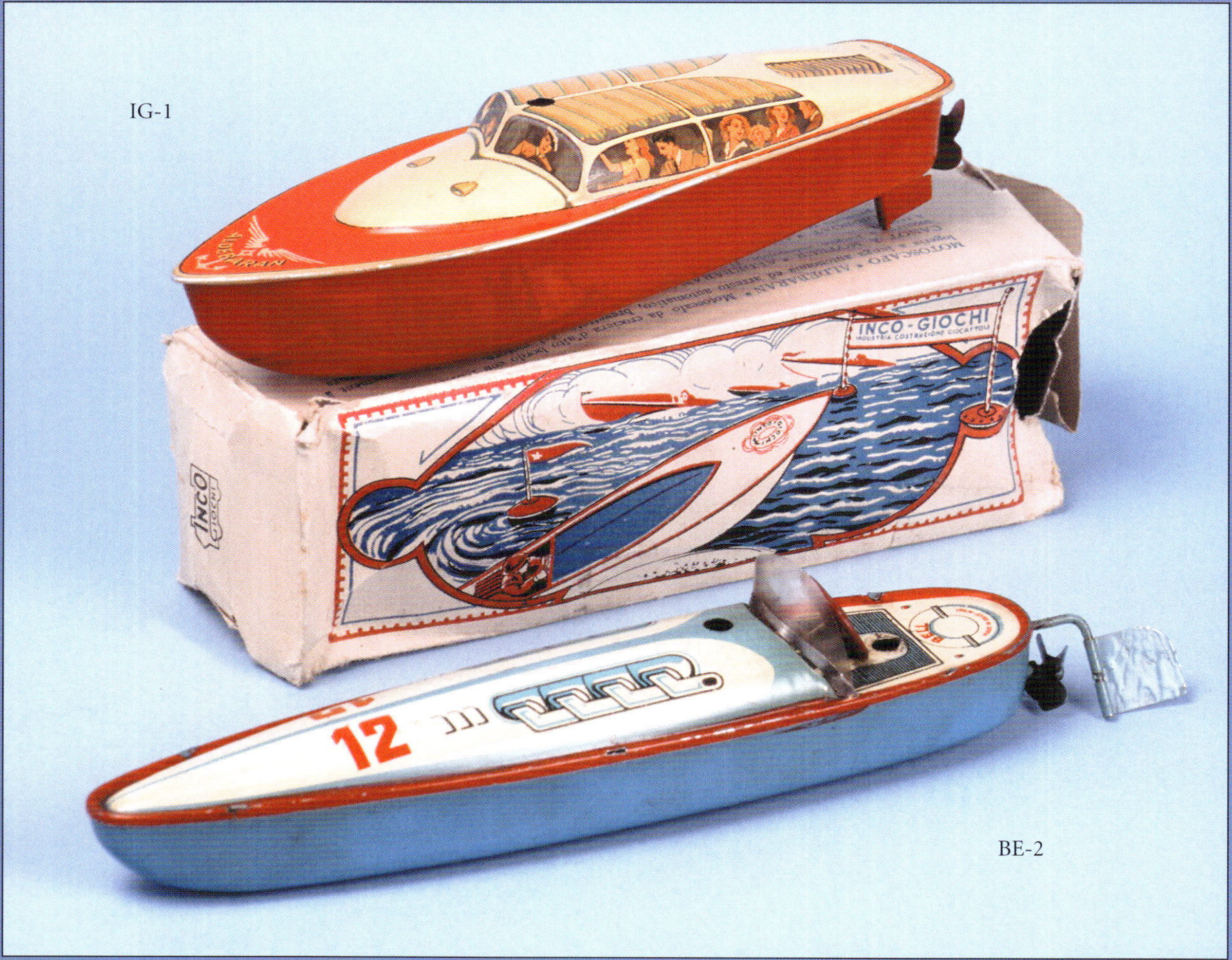

Bell & INGAP (Inco-Giochi)

Top: (IG-1) **1950's, 7″ clockwork cabin cruiser.**
Bottom: (BE-2) **1950's, 8″ speedboat.**

NAME	LOCATION	DATES	FOUNDER	PAGE
Bell	Milan	1919-?	Vittorio Belloni	176
INGAP	Padova	–	–	176
Monteleone	–	–	–	177
Ventura	Treviso, Preganziol and in 1951 Torno	1936-1982	Angelo Ventura	177-178

(VA-7) 1950's 32″ sailboat *Squalo*.

(MTE-1) **1960, 39″ battery powered plastic liner *Porto Alegre*. This ship has the wonderfully styled outline of the Italian liners of the period and is reminiscent of the *Andria Doria*.**

(VA-2) 1950's, 35″ battery powered plastic liner *United States*. This is one of the more impressive representations of the famous United States Lines trans-Atlantic liner. On her maiden voyage from New York on July 3, 1952, she took the Blue Riband by attaining an average speed between Ambrose light and Bishop Rocks of 35.39 knots. The liner was the fastest commercial ship ever built and rumored to be capable of over 40 knots.

Wooden hulled clockwork
ships of the 1940's and 1950's.
Rear to front:
(VA-5) 18″ cruiser *TI-7*,
(VA-3) 27″ aircraft carrier *Vis*,
(VA-1) 14″ ocean liner.
The liner has a metal
superstructure while the
warships are mostly wood
except for railings
and AA guns.

178

1950's battery powered plastic hulled warships.
Rear: (VA-6) 22″ aircraft carrier *Tigre*.
Front: (VA-4) 35″ cruiser *Los Angeles*.
Ventura combined several materials, such as wood (the turrets),
metal (AA guns, cranes, mast) and plastic on their ships.

Russian Manufacturer

UK-91

J-10

Leningrad Metallurgical Factory

Copied almost exactly from the JEP 0 (J-10), and with comparable quality, this Russian version (UK-91) displays graphics on the box which show children playing in the Neva River in St. Petersburg. In the background are the Peter-Paul Fortress and the Naval Museum bracketed by rostral columns. The LM trademark on the box end is that of the Leningrad Metallurgical Factory.

Spanish Manufacturer

Paya

Very similar to Kellermann's #226/7, these two 9″ clockwork floor toys were made in the 1930's.
Left: (PA-6) *Espana.*
Right: (PA-7) *Eagle.*

PA-6

PA-7

(PA-2)
14″ clockwork rower.

(PA-1) 1930's, 8″ clockwork outboard speedboat.

PA-1

PA-2

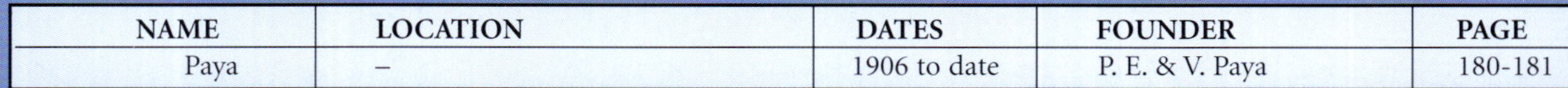

NAME	LOCATION	DATES	FOUNDER	PAGE
Paya	–	1906 to date	P. E. & V. Paya	180-181

PA-5

(PA-5) **1990's, 13″ clockwork battleship. Accurately reproduced ship from the 1930's.**

181

(PA-4) **13″ clockwork ocean liner.**

PA-4

Toy Ship Index with Price Guide

Ref. No.	Page	Type	Cond.	Est. Value
Althof-Bergmann				
AB-1	2	Paddle-wheeler	E	$12,500
Am.Toyland Creators				
ATC-1	10	Submarine	E	$100
Arnold				
A-1	67	Liner	E	$350
A-2	67	Liner	E	$1,000
A-3	67	Liner	E	$750
A-4	67	Liner	E	$2,400
A-5	69	Set	E	$800
A-6	66	Liner	E	$500
A-7	65	Liner	E	$400
A-8	65	Liner	E	$400
A-9	65	Liner	E	$200
A-10	68	Liner	E	$350
A-11	67	Liner	E	$900
A-12	68	Liner	E	$550
A-13	68	Liner	E	$300
A-14	68	Liner	E	$250
A-15	67	Liner	E	$250
A-16	68	Freighter	E	$350
A-17	74	Motorboat	E	$100
A-18	71	Battleship	LN	$850
A-19	72	Submarine	E	$400
A-20	72	Submarine	E	$500
A-21	72	Submarine	E	$450
A-22	71	Submarine	VG	$250
A-23	71	Submarine	E	$350
A-24	71	Submarine	VG	$400
A-25	73	Speedboat	E	$400
A-26	73	Speedboat	E	$500
A-28	73	Airboat	E	$800
A-29	73	Outboard	E	$1,000
A-30	70	Cruiser	E	$350
A-31	72	Submarine	VG	$200
A-32	71	Submarine	E	$400
A-33	65	Liner	E	$450
A-34	65	Liner	G	$200
A-35	65	Liner	E	$250
A-36	65	Liner	E	$400
A-37	66	Liner	E	$685
A-38	67	Liner	E	$3,000
A-39	74	Canoe	E	$500
A-41	74	Rowboat	E	$750
A-42	71	Battleship	VG	$250
A-44	68	Tug	G	$250
A-45	71	Destroyer	E	$225
A-46	71	Battleship	E	$250
A-47	68	Paddle-wheeler	E	$500
A-48	70	Gunboat	VG	$347
A-49	66	Liner	E	$982
A-50	74	Rowboat	E	$600
A-51	67	Liner	E	$800
A-52	65	Liner	E	$900
A-53	67	Liner	E	$1,600
A-54	67	Liner	E	$1,000
A-55	67	Liner	E	$500
A-56	66	Liner	E	$2,500
A-57	65	Liner	E	$2,000
A-58	74	Speedboat	E	$250
A-59	68	Liner	G	$160
A-60	65	Liner	G	$250
A-61	66	Liner	E	$500
A-62	65	Liner	VG	$150
A-63	65	Liner	VG	$110
A-64	66	Liner	E	$250
A-65	70	Cruiser	G	$450
A-66	67	Liner	E	$400
A-67	68	Paddle-wheeler	E	$500
A-68	70	Battleship	E	$500
A-69	71	Battleship	G	$300
A-70	70	Battleship	G	$300
A-71	66	Liner	G	$400
A-72	64	Liner	E	$1,000

Ref. No.	Page	Type	Cond.	Est. Value
A-73	69	Liner	E	$125
A-74	69	Sightseeing	E	$125
A-75	74	Cabin Cruiser	E	$100
A-76	74	Cabin Cruiser	E	$100
A-77	74	Rowboat	E	$600
A-78	73	Air Boat	E	$600
A-79	66	Liner	E	$300
A-80	68	Liner	VG	$350
A-81	73	Speedboat	E	$500
A-83	71	Battleship	E	$198
Artwood				
AR-1	3	Set of 5 Sailboats	E	$100
Baker & Bennett				
BB-1	3	Exploding Boat	VG	$200
Bell(Italy)				
BE-2	176	Speedboat	VG	$100
Bell(UK)				
BE-1	41	Puzzle	E	$40
Bethune, H				
BNE-1	53	Liner, Biscuit Tin	G	$300
Bing				
B-1	92	Ferry	G	$4,500
B-2	92	Ferry	VG	$3,500
B-3	92	Ferry	VG	$3,500
B-4	77	Liner	E	$1,800
B-5	78	Liner	E	$10,000
B-6	78	Liner	VG	$1,500
B-7	79	Liner	E	$4,000
B-8	83	Torpedo Boat	VG	$1,000
B-9	93	Tug	E	$2,500
B-10	93	Fire Boat	G	$1,500
B-11	77	Liner	G	$1,000
B-12	76	Liner	VG	$9,000
B-13	85	Gunboat	E	$3,500
B-14	86	Cruiser	E	$2,800
B-15	88	Battleship	E	$3,000
B-16	85	Armored Cruiser	E	$3,200

Ref. No.	Page	Type	Cond.	Est. Value
B-17	84	Gunboat	E	$3,500
B-18	82	Gunboat	E	$500
B-19	81	Torpedo Boat	E	$5,000
B-20	82	Destroyer	E	$7,500
B-21	82	Torpedo Boat	E	$2,500
B-22	80	Torpedo Boat	VG	$3,500
B-23	83	Torpedo Boat	VG	$1,200
B-24	83	Torpedo Boat	E	$3,000
B-25	91	Submarine	VG	$500
B-26	91	Submarine	LN	$700
B-27	91	Submarine	G	$200
B-28	90	Submarine	E	$2,500
B-29	90	Submarine	P	$750
B-30	90	Submarine	E	$750
B-31	97	Speedboat	E	$2,000
B-32	96	Speedboat	LN	$750
B-33	93	Speedboat	E	$500
B-34	95	Paddle-Wheeler	E	$1,000
B-35	95	River Boat	VG	$3,000
B-36	94	River Boat	LN	$4,000
B-37	95	River Boat	E	$7,000
B-38	77	Liner	E	$2,800
B-39	79	Liner	VG	$600
B-41	78	Liner	E	$6,000
B-42	80	Torpedo Boat	E	$4,000
B-43	81	Torpedo Boat	E	$1,500
B-44	84	Torpedo Boat	E	$2,000
B-45	85	Gunboat	E	$750
B-46	76	Liner	E	$3,200
B-47	85	Armored Cruiser	VG	$1,300
B-48	75	Liner	E	$8,500
B-49	78	Liner	E	$3,000
B-50	96	Speedboat	VG	$325
B-51	97	Speedboat	G	$700
B-52	77	Liner	E	$2,800
B-53	96	Sailboat	E	$3,500
B-54	88	Battleship	E	$3,500

Ref. No.	Page	Type	Cond.	Est. Value
B-55	94	River Boat	E	$2,500
B-56	76	Liner	E	$1,060
B-57	79	Liner	E	$250
B-58	82	Destroyer	E	$6,500
B-59	86	Cruiser	E	$4,500
B-60	82	Destroyer	E	$7,000
B-61	77	Liner	E	$12,000
B-62	79	Liner	VG	$440
B-63	97	Speedboat	VG	$3,500
B-64	85	Armored Cruiser	VG	$3,500
B-65	81	Torpedo Boat	E	$3,250
B-66	93	Fire Boat	E	$1,100
B-67	96	Speedboat	E	$650
B-68	91	Submarine	LN	$2,350
B-69	92	Paddle-wheeler	P	$75
B-70	91	Submarine	E	$225
B-72	91	Submarine	E	$200
B-73	85	Battleship	E	$1,000
B-74	95	Paddle-wheeler	E	$800
B-75	86	Cruiser	E	$1,800
B-76	88	Battleship	E	$1,700
B-77	79	Liner	E	$1,200
B-78	76	Liner	E	$750
B-79	77	Liner	E	$4,000
B-80	88	Battleship	E	$3,000
B-81	86	Cruiser	E	$6,000
B-82	92	Ferry	E	$1,000
B-83	81	Torpedo Boat	VG	$7,500
B-84	77	Liner	E	$3,500
B-85	87	Gunboat	E	$8,500
B-86	91	Submarine	E	$800
B-87	84	Torpedo Boat	VG	$1,000
B-89	79	Liner	E	$550
B-90	79	Liner	E	$1,500
B-91	76	Liner	E	$11,000
B-92	79	Liner	E	$1,000
B-93	92	Motorboat	G	$100
B-94	91	Submarine	E	$250
B-95	76	Liner	E	$1,500

Ref. No.	Page	Type	Cond.	Est. Value
B-96	79	Liner	VG	$350
B-97	88	Battleship	E	$750
B-98	93, 95	Speedboat	E	$500
B-99	88	Battleship	E	$1,000
B-100	78	Liner	E	$1,100
B-101	78, 93	Liner	E	$375
B-102	87	Battleship	E	$4,000
B-103	87	Gunboat	E	$10,000
B-104	86	Cruiser	VG	$3,500
B-105	77	Liner	E	$1,155
B-106	97	Speedboat	E	$1,210
B-107	80	Torpedo Boat	E	$3,000
B-108	82	Torpedo Boat	E	$1,200
B-109	76	Liner	E	$4,500
B-110	80	Torpedo Boat	VG	$4,000
B-111	95	Paddle-wheeler	E	$950
B-112	76, 93	Liner	E	$88
B-113	95	Rowboat	E	$1,375
B-114	93	Liner	VG	$200
B-115	93	Paddle-wheeler	E	$750
B-116	79	Liner	E	$2,000
B-117	93	Fireboat	G	$200
B-118	89	Battleship	E	$15,000
B-119	95	B & B'House	G	$550
B-120	84	Gunboat	LN	$3,300
B-123	89	Battleship	E	$20,000

Bliss

Ref. No.	Page	Type	Cond.	Est. Value
BL-1	3	Battleship	E	$1,000

Bonnet (Vebe)

Ref. No.	Page	Type	Cond.	Est. Value
BV-1	51	Gunboat	E	$200
BV-2	51	Liner	E	$350
BV-3	53	Liner	VG	$250

Boucher

Ref. No.	Page	Type	Cond.	Est. Value
BU-1	4	Speedboat	E	$1,000
BU-3	4	Outboard	E	$600
BU-5	4	Sailboat	VG	$275

Bowman

Ref. No.	Page	Type	Cond.	Est. Value
BN-1	40	Speedboat	VG	$400
BN-2	40	Speedboat	E	$700

Ref. No.	Page	Type	Cond.	Est. Value
BN-3	40	Speedboat	E	$1,000
BN-4	40	Speedboat	G	$500
BN-5	40	Cabin Cruiser	E	$1,800
Bramwell-Smith				
BS-1	4	Paddle-wheeler	VG	$6,050
Brandt				
BT-1	98	Build-A-Boat	VG	$400
Brown, Geo				
BR-1	5	Monitor	VG	$12,500
BR-2	5	Paddle-wheeler	E	$16,000
BR-3	5	Paddle-wheeler	G	$18,000
BR-5	5	Paddle-wheeler	VG	$10,500
Büchner				
BH-1	98	Paddle-wheeler	E	$5,000
BH-2	98	Sailboat W/Soldr.	G	$450
BH-3	98	Pinnace	G	$800
Cappel & Macdonald				
CM-1	6	Boat Builder	G	$50
Carette				
C-1	100	Liner	VG	$350
C-2	100	Liner	VG	$1,000
C-3	100	Liner	VG	$1,800
C-4	100	Liner	VG	$1,200
C-5	102	Torpedo Boat	VG	$400
C-7	103	Yacht	VG	$2,500
C-8	103,166	Riverboat	E	$4,000
C-12	104	Riverboat	VG	$300
C-13	99	Ocean Steamer	G	$500
C-14	166	Riverboat	E	$4,000
C-15	105	Speedboat	G	$670
C-17	105	Speedboat	VG	$250
C-18	103	Yacht	E	$3,000
C-19	102	Torpedo Boat	G	$600
C-20	102	Battleship	E	
C-21	100	Liner	E	$1,000
C-22	104,105	Riverboat	E	$800
C-23	99, 110	Liner	E	$2,000
C-24	100	Liner	VG	$220
C-25	101,113	Cruiser	G	$1,000
C-26	101	Gunboat	E	$2,500

Ref. No.	Page	Type	Cond.	Est. Value
C-27	101	Gunboat	G	$200
C-29	105	Yacht	G	$200
C-30	105	Speedboat	F	$250
C-31	105	Speedboat Set	E	$1,900
C-32	104	Riverboat	E	$900
Cass, N.D., Co.				
CS-1	6	Liner	E	$40
CS-2	6	Sailboat	E	$50
CS-3	6	Tug	E	$40
CS-4	6	Liner	E	$120
Chein				
CH-1	7	Motorboat	E	$150
CH-2	7	Motorboat	E	$75
CH-3	7	Cabin Cruiser	E	$200
CH-4	7	Sailboat	E	$170
CH-5	7	Sailboat	E	$100
CH-6	7	Speedboat	G	$75
CH-7	7	Speedboat	VG	$50
Codeg (UK)				
CG-1	41	Launch	E	$200
Cohn				
CN-1	8	Boat Fleet	E	$200
CN-2	8	Cabin Cruiser	E	$65
CN-3	8	Sand Boat	E	$100
Consolidated Toy Mfg.				
CD-1	8	Sailboat		$25
CD-2	8	Sailboat	E	$25
Converse				
CE-1	9	Launch	F	$660
CE-2	9	Armored Cruiser	G	$1,000
CE-4	9	Sailboat	VG	$200
CE-5	9	Sailboat	G	$80
CE-6	9	Sailboat	E	$300
CE-7	9	Sailboat	G	$200
CE-9	9	Sailboat	G	$150
Crawford, Wm.				
CF-1	49	Liner	E	$2,200
Dent				
DT-1	8	Battleship	E	$7,500

Ref. No.	Page	Type	Cond.	Est. Value
Distler				
DR-1	106	Liner	VG	$600
DR-2	106	Speedboat	E	$495
DR-3	106	Battleship	E	$330
Einfalt (Kosmos)				
ET-1	106	Liner	E	$350
Falk				
FK-1	107	Liner	E	$2,500
FK-2	101,108	Battleship	VG	$2,500
FK-3	122	Yacht	VG	$500
FK-4	107	Liner	E	$580
FK-5	107	Liner	E	$400
FK-6	107	Riverboat	E	$5,500
Fallows				
FS-1	10	Paddle-wheeler	E	$7,500
FS-2	10	Paddle-wheeler	G	$3,500
Fischer				
FR-1	108	Liner	VG	$200
FR-2	108	Launch	E	$935
FR-3	108	Gunboat	G	$55
FR-4	108	Battleship	E	$577
FR-5	108	Battleship	E	$412
Fleischmann				
F-1	112	Liner	E	$750
F-2	112	Liner	E	$3,000
F-3	119	Tanker	E	$1,500
F-4	119	Tanker	E	$1,000
F-5	119	Freighter	E	$1,000
F-6	118	Liner	E	$350
F-7	118	Liner	E	$350
F-8	111,112	Liner	E	$525
F-9	112	Liner	E	$500
F-10	111	Liner	E	$400
F-11	111	Line	E	$750
F-12	111	Liner	E	$1,000
F-13	110	Liner	E	$1,800
F-14	111	Liner	E	$2,500
F-15	111	Liner	E	$5,000
F-16	109	Liner	E	$8,000
F-17	111	Liner	E	$3,500
F-18	111	Liner	E	$3,000
F-19	111	Liner	E	$1,800
F-20	118	Tug	E	$250
F-20A	118	Barge	E	$800
F-20B	118	Barge W/Covers	E	$150
F-20C	118	Barge W/Crane	E	$150
F-21	112	Motorboat	E	$125
F-22	119	Fire Boat	VG	$800
F-23	119	House Boat	E	$3,500
F-24	122	Yacht	VG	$1,200
F-25	118	Ferry	E	$2,500
F-26	115	Battleship	E	$3,000
F-27	114	Battleship	VG	$5,000
F-28	114	Battleship	VG	$1,500
F-29	114	Battleship	VG	$1,500
F-30	114	Battleship	VG	$600
F-31	115	Destroyer	E	$1,800
F-32	116	Submarine	VG	$440
F-33	117	Submarine	VG	$800
F-34	117	Submarine	E	$1,500
F-35	116	Submarine	G	$250
F-36	116,117	Submarine	G	$350
F-37	116	Submarine	G	$400
F-38	116	Submarine	G	$400
F-40	113	Torpedo Boat	E	$1,000
F-41	113	Coastal Cruiser	VG	$1,600
F-42	119	House Boat	E	$825
F-43	114	Battleship	E	$1,300
F-45	119	Fire Boat	E	$800
F-46	114	Battleship	E	$3,000
F-47	111	Liner	E	$300
F-48	115	Destroyer	E	$900
F-49	121	Paddle-wheeler	G	$4,620
F-50	120	Paddle-wheeler	G	$2,080
F-51	115	Destroyer	E	$500
F-52	120	Paddle-wheeler	GE	$4,000
F-53	110	Liner	E	$840
F-54	114	Battleship	G	$2,500

186

Ref. No.	Page	Type	Cond.	Est. Value
F-55	122	Riverboat	VG	$816
F-56	110	Liner	E	$4,000
F-57	111	Liner	E	$900
F-58	109	Liner	E	$8,000
F-59	110	Liner	E	$1,800
F-60	115	Battleship	E	$2,000
F-61	118	Ferry	E	$3,500
F-62	122	Riverboat	E	$2,500
F-63	120	Paddle-wheeler	E	$2,400
F-64	110	Liner	E	$2,000
F-65	110	Liner	E	$250
F-66	116	Submarine	E	$300
F-67	116	Submarine	VG	$150
F-68	116	Submarine	G	$100
F-69	99,110	Liner	E	$900
F-70	123	Sailboat	E	$1,800
F-71	113	Coastal Cruiser	G	$665
F-72	121	Paddle-wheeler	G	$350
F-73	113	Coastal Cruiser	VG	$1,800
F-74	110	Liner	E	$900
F-75	113	Torpedo Boat	E	$800
F-76	121	Paddle-wheeler	E	$850
F-77	111	Liner	E	$250
F-78	110	Liner	G	$250
F-79	114	Battleship	E	$500
F-80	111	Liner	VG	$450
F-81	111	Liner	E	$900
F-82	124	Gunboat & Tower	VG	$800
F-83	121	Paddle-wheeler	E	$1,200
F-84	120	Paddle-wheeler	E	$1,000
F-85	111	Liner	E	$300
F-86	118	Cargo	G	$290
F-87	111	Liner	E	$200
F-88	120	Paddle-wheeler	VG	$600
F-89	110	Liner	E	$4,000
F-90	111	Liner	E	$4,000
F-91	113	Coastal Cruiser	E	$750
F-92	124	Lighthouse/Boat	G	$250
F-93	118	Liner	E	$264

Ref. No.	Page	Type	Cond.	Est. Value
F-94	113	Coastal Cruiser	E	$550
F-95	110	Liner	VG	$500
F-96	101,113	Gunboat	E	$400
F-97	124	Gunboat	G	$100
F-98	124	Gunboat	G	$100
F-99	123	Excursion	E	$300
F-100	124	Boat/Duck Set	VG	$600
F-101	120	Steamer	VG	$275
F-102	124	River Boat	E	$600
F-103	124	River Boat	E	$500
F-104	120	Paddle-wheeler	VG	$1,500
F-105	118	Crane Boat	VG	$100
F-106	120	Steamer	E	$300
F-107	110	Liner	E	$500
F-109	116	Submarine	E	$700
Flory				
FY-1	41	Submarine	E	$150
FY-2	41	Speedboat	E	$100
Fulton				
FN-1	10	Submarine Set 3	G	$100
Gescha				
GR-1	125	Sailboat	E	$300
GR-2	125	Sailboat	E	$450
Gil				
GL-1	52	Torpedo Boat	E	$500
GL-2	52	Submarine	E	$600
GL-3	52	Cabin Cruiser	E	$300
GL-4	52	Torpedo Boat	E	$600
Gilbert				
GT-1	10	Submarine	G	$200
Gobar				
GB-1	10	Speedboat	E	$200
Greppert & Kelch				
GK-1	125	Liner	E	$400
GK-2	125	Liner	E	$1,200
Gunthermann				
GN-1	126	Racing Scull-1	E	$4,600
GN-2	126	Racing Scull-2	E	$4,887
GN-3	126	Racing Scull-4	E	$7,475

187

Ref. No.	Page	Type	Cond.	Est. Value
GN-4	126	Racing Scull-8	E	$12,947
(IR-5	132	Battleship	E	$1,500)
Hess				
H-1	128	Riverboat	VG	$350
H-2	129	Sailboat	F	$100
H-3	129	Sailboat	E	$500
H-4	129	Sailboat	E	$300
H-5	127	Gunboat	VG	$200
H-6	127	Gunboat	VG	$200
H-7	127	Gunboat	E	$350
H-8	127	Gunboat	VG	$350
H-9	127	Submarine	E	$100
H-10	127	Gunboat Set	VG	$1,500
H-11	128	Battleship Set	E	$300
H-12	127	Destroyer	E	$400
H-13	128	Battleship	E	$375
H-14	129	Speedboat	VG	$500
H-15	129	Steam Launch	E	$165
H-16	127	Steam Launch	E	$253
H-18	127	Steamer	E	$100
Heyde				
HE-1	130	Set of 10 Ships	E	$1,000
HE-2	130	Set of 8 Ships	E	$2,750
HE-3	131	Set of 6 Ships	E	$3,500
HE-5	130	3 Cannon w/Sailors	E	$2,000
Horndlein				
HN-1	131	Submarine	VG	$400
HN-2	131	Submarine	E	$150
HN-3	131	Submarine	E	$75
Husch				
HH-1	50	Liner	E	$400
HH-2	50	Liner	E	$300
Ideal				
ID-1	10	Submarine	G	$500
Inco-Giochi				
IG-1	176	Cabin Cruiser	E	$150
Issmayer				
IR-1	98	Launch	F	$300
IR-2	98	Launch	E	$100
IR-4	132	Sailboat w/Boy	E	$3,300
IR-5	132	Battleship	E	$1,500
Ives				
I-1	12	Submarine	E	$400
I-2	12	Submarine	E	$600
I-3	13	Patrol Boat	E	$1,000
I-4	13	Patrol Boat	G	$1,000
I-5	13	Patrol Boat	VG	$1,500
I-6	13	Speedboat	E	$800
I-7	13	Speedboat	VG	$600
I-8	13	Speedboat	VG	$800
I-9	12	Tug	G	$900
I-11	12	Tug	VG	$650
I-12	12	Destroyer	E	$1,500
I-13	12	Destroyer	E	$600
I-14	12	Destroyer	E	$800
I-15	14	Freighter	E	$1,000
I-16	14	Freighter	VG	$600
I-17	14	Freighter	VG	$1,200
I-18	14	Freighter	VG	$750
I-19	14	Freighter	VG	$750
I-20	15	River Boat	VG	$2,000
I-21	11	Rowboat	E	$7,500
I-22	12	Destroyer	E	$850
I-23	13	Patrol Boat	VG	$900
I-25	14	Liner	VG	$1,500
I-26	14	Liner	E	$1,500
I-27	14	Liner	E	$650
I-28	13	Patrol Boat	VG	$600
I-29	12	Tug	VG	$800
I-30	12	Submarine	E	$600
I-31	13	Patrol Boat	VG	$750
I-32	12	Destroyer	G	$500
I-33	14	Liner	E	$1,500
I-34	13	Speedboat	E	$650
I-35	14	Liner	G	$1,200
I-36	12	Destroyer	E	$1,000

Ref. No.	Page	Type	Cond.	Est. Value
JEP				
J-1	55	Submarine	E	$750
J-2	54	Liner	VG	$375
J-3	54	Torpedo Boat	VG	$1,500
J-4	55	Submarine	E	$500
J-5	55	Speedboat	E	$450
J-6	55	Speedboat	E	$400
J-7	55	Speedboat	E	$400
J-8	55	Speedboat	E	$400
J-9	55	Speedboat	E	$400
J-10	55	Speedboat	E	$600
J-11	55	Speedboat	E	$400
J-12	54	Liner	E	$2,500
J-13	54	Cruiser	E	$300
J-14	55	Speedboat	E	$250
J-15	54	Liner	E	$800
J-16	55	Speedboat	E	$350
J-17	55	Speedboat	E	$300
J-18	55	Submarine	E	$400
J-19	55	Cabin Cruiser	E	$200
Jouet Charlys				
JC-1	56	Battleship	E	$250
JRD (France)				
JD-1	56	Torpedo Boat	E	$250
JD-2	56	Cabin Cruiser	E	$250
Kellermann				
CK-1	133	Liner	G	$150
CK-2	133	Liner	E	$500
CK-4	133	Battleship	E	$300
CK-5	133	Speedboat	E	$300
CK-6	133	Liner	E	$468
CK-7	49, 133	Paddle-wheeler	G	$100
CK-8	133	Liner	E	$110
CK-10	133	Paddle-wheeler	VG	$121
CK-11	133	Liner	E	$1,200
CK-12	133	Liner	E	$660
Kellner				
KLR-1	134	Speedboat	E	$900
KLR-2	134	Speedboat	VG	$1,000

Ref. No.	Page	Type	Cond.	Est. Value
KLR-3	134	Speedboat	E	$700
Keystone				
K-1	18	A/C Carrier	E	$200
K-2	18	Exploding Boat	E	$200
K-3	18	Rocket Ship	G	$75
K-4	18	Battleship	VG	$65
K-5	18	Submarine	E	$50
K-6	19	Tug	E	$75
K-7	19	Speedboat	E	$100
K-8	19	Tug	E	$100
K-9	19	Barge	E	$20
K-10	16	Liner	VG	$350
K-11	18	Rocket Ship	E	$220
K-12	17	Sailboat	E	$150
K-13	18	A/C Carrier	E	$50
K-14	18	Cruiser	E	$50
K-15	18	Submarine	VG	$10
K-16	17	Speedboat	E	$100
K-17	19	Tug	VG	$20
K-18	17	Fishing Boat	E	$100
K-19	19	Ferry	E	$150
K-20	19	Tug w/Barge	E	$150
K-21	18	Radar Rkt. Ship	E	$100
K-22	17	Sailboat	E	$35
K-23	19	Speedboat	E	$150
K-24	16	Boat Hse & Boat	E	$350
K-25	17	Tub N Table Fleet	E	$100
Lefevre, E.F.				
LE-1	58	Paddle-wheeler	E	$2,500
LE-2	58	Paddle-wheeler	E	$4,100
LE-3	57	Paddle-wheeler	E	$7,500
LE-4	58	Gunboat	VG	$2,800
LE-5	58	Paddle-wheeler	E	$3,500
Lehmann				
LN-1	135	Battleship	E	$1,000
LN-2	135	Torpedo Boat	VG	$900
LN-3	135	Aircraft Carrier	E	$75
LN-4	135	Liner	E	$75
LN-5	135	Railferry	E	$75

189

Ref. No.	Page	Type	Cond.	Est. Value
LN-6	135	Oil Tanker	E	$75
LN-7	135	Freighter	E	$75
LN-8	135	Liner	E	$75
Leningrad Metallurgical Factory				
UK-91	179	Speedboat	E	$200
Levy, Georg				
LG-1	134	Liner	VG	$150
LG-2	134	Liner	E	$743
LG-3	134	Liner	E	$908
LG-4	134	Liner	G	$121
LG-5	134	Rowboat	E	$150
LG-6	134	Rowboat	G	$577
Liberty				
LY-1	20	Fireboat	E	$750
LY-2	20	Speedboat	E	$375
LY-4	20	Riverboat	E	$230
LY-5	20	Tug	E	$250
LY-6	20	A/C Carrier	E	$800
Lindstrom				
L-1	21	Ferry	VG	$460
L-2	21	Liner	E	$490
L-3	21	Speedboat	G	$175
L-4	21	Speedboat	VG	$175
L-5	21	Speedboat	E	$71.50
L-6	21	Speedboat	E	$186
L-7	21	Torpedo Boat	E	$70.
L-8	21	Liner	G	$35
L-9	20	Rowboat/Outboard	E	$825
L-10	20	Speedboat	E	$75
L-11	20	Outboard	E	$100
L-12	20	Speedboat	E	$150
L-13	21	Show Boat	VG	$99
L-14	21	Speedboat	G	$41
L-15	21	Speedboat	VG	$264
Lionel				
LL-1	22	Speedboat	E	$600
LL-2	22	Speedboat	LN	$2,100
M & P Manufacturing. Co.				
M&P-1	23	Fireboat	E	$75

Ref. No.	Page	Type	Cond.	Est. Value
M&P-2	23	Freighter	G	$20
M&P-3	23	Tug	G	$20
M&P-4	23	Liner	E	$75
Märklin				
M-1	149	Battleship	E	$26,000
M-2	150	Battleship	E	$12,000
M-3	150	Battleship	VG	$12,000
M-4	150	Battleship	VG	$5,000
M-5	150	Battleship	VG	$5,000
M-6	151	Submarine	E	$1,800
M-8	151	Submarine	VG	$1,200
M-9	151	Submarine	E	$1,100
M-10	151	Submarine	E	$500
M-11	146	Cruiser	E	$17,500
M-12	141	Liner	E	$7,500
M-13	141	Liner	E	$9,000
M-14	142	Liner	VG	$18,000
M-15	155	Yacht	E	$17,000
M-16	144	Paddle-wheeler	E	$21,000
M-17	150	Battleship	E	$5,000
M-18	144	Paddle-wheeler	E	$17,000
M-19	151	Submarine	E	$6,000
M-20	151	Submarine	E	$9,000
M-21	138	Liner	E	$36,000
M-22	142	Liner	E	$20,000
M-23	147	Gunboat	E	$11,000
M-24	141	Liner	E	$4,100
M-25	147	Torpedo Boat	E	$3,500
M-26	151	Submarine	E	$1,000
M-27	141	Liner	E	$6,000
M-28	150	Battleship	E	$6,000
M-29	141	Liner	E	$3,000
M-30	143	Liner	F	$8,000
M-31	151	Submarine	E	$600
M-32	146	Cruiser	E	$29,000
M-33	154	Riverboat	E	$3,000
M-34	155	Launch	E	$5,500
M-35	148	Battleship	E	$27,500
M-36	140,141	Liner	E	$35,000

Ref. No.	Page	Type	Cond.	Est. Value
M-37	139	Liner	E	$35,000
M-38	155	Launch	E	$2,000
M-39	155	Yacht	E	$18,000
M-41	144	Liner	E	$3,000
M-42	136	Liner	E	$70,000
M-43	152	Paddle-wheeler	E	$110,000
M-44	147	Torpedo Boat	E	$6,000
M-45	136,141	Liner	E	$3,500
M-46	140,141	Liner	E	$1,800
M-47	140	Liner	E	$8,000
M-48	154	Motor Yacht	E	$7,500
M-49	146	Battleship	E	$35,000
M-50	144	Liner	E	$8,500
M-51	149	Battleship	VG	$2,000
M-52	144	Liner	E	$2,000
M-53	154	Riverboat	E	$7,500
M-54	155	Launch	E	$750
M-55	140	Liner	E	$14,000
M-56	151	Submarine	E	$5,000
M-57	151	Submarine	E	$1,000
M-58	143	Liner	E	$25,000
M-59	145	Battleship	E	$55,000
M-60	150	Battleship	E	$12,000
Marx				
MX-1	22	Liner	NM	$150
MX-2	22	Battleship	E	$150
MX-5	22	Set of 3 Ships	E	$50
MX-6	22	Cabin Cruiser	E	$25
MX-8	22	Liner	E	$25
Meccano				
ME-1	42	Liner	VG	$80
ME-2	43	Speedboat	E	$250
ME-3	42	Speedboat	E	$200
ME-4	43	Speedboat	NM	$300
ME-5	43	Speedboat	E	$350
ME-6	43	Speedboat	E	$535
ME-7	43	Speedboat	G	$125
ME-10	42	Speedboat	E	$135
ME-11	42	Cabin Cruiser	E	$400
ME-12	42	Speedboat	VG	$300
ME-13	42	Limo Boat	E	$400
Meier				
MR-1	156	Launch	E	$1,000
MR-2	156	Paddle-wheeler	E	$165
MR-3	156	Steamer	E	$100.
MR-4	156	Liner	E	$468
MR-5	156	Sailboat	E	$1,000
MR-6	156	Battleship	E	$500
MR-7	156	Speedboat	VG	$275
Memo (France)				
MM-1	53	Liner	E	$600
Mengel				
MG-1	23	Speedboat	E	$500
MG-2	23	Speedboat	E	$275
Mignot (C.B.G.)				
MT-1	59	Sea Battle	E	$2,000
MT-2	59	Sea Battle	E	$800
Milbro (UK)				
MO-1	44	Sailboat	E	$450
Mohr & Krauss				
MK-1	156	Gunboat	VG	$200
MK-2	156	Gunboat	E	$300
MK-3	156	Battleship	VG	$900
MK-4	156	Battleship	VG	$500
Monteleone				
MTE-1	177	Liner	E	$75
Nova (France)				
MFP-1	59	Speedboat	E	$300
NY Cal (Liberty)				
NY-1	22	Speedboat	E	$95
NY-2	22	Outboard	E	$150
NY-3	22	Outboard	E	$230
Ohio Art				
OA-1	23	Speedboat	NM	$50
OA-2	23	Speedboat	E	$50
Orkin				
OR-1	26	Liner	VG	$700
OR-2	25	Cruiser	E	$900

Ref. No.	Page	Type	Cond.	Est. Value
OR-3	24	Battleship	VG	$2,585
OR-4	24	Battle Cruiser	E	$1,500
OR-5	26	Liner	E	$800
OR-6	26	Speedboat	E	$350
OR-7	24	Battleship	E	$1,200
OR-8	24	Battleship	E	$3,200
OR-9	25	Destroyer	E	$2,250
OR-10	26	Patrol Boat	E	$1,700
OR-11	25	Chaser	E	$1,000
OR-12	26	Launch	VG	$800
OR-13	25	Battleship	E	$1,500
OR-14	26	Battleship	E	$7,200
OR-15	25	Battleship	E	$2,500
Orobr				
O-1	157	Battleship	E	$2,000
O-2	157	Paddle-wheeler	E	$750
O-3	157	Cruiser	E	$1,000
O-4	157	Liner	E	$750
O-5	157	Destroyer	E	$1,500
Paya				
PA-1	180	Speedboat	E	$150
PA-2	180	Rowboat	E	$150
PA-4	181	Liner	E	$150
PA-5	181	Battleship	E	$150
PA-6	180	Liner	E	$550
PA-7	180	Liner	VG	$300
Plank				
EP-1	159	Torpedo Boat	VG	$2,000
EP-2	159	Submarine	E	$2,000
EP-3	158	Riverboat	G	$1,800
EP-4	158	Riverboat	E	$300
EP-5	158	Riverboat	E	$800
EP-6	158	Riverboat	E	$800
EP-7	159	Torpedo & Tube	E	$1,500
EP-8	159	Submarine	E	$1,400
EP-9	159	Submarine	E	$1,000
EP-10	158	Air-Pontoon Boat	E	$2,000

Ref. No.	Page	Type	Cond.	Est. Value
Radiguet				
R-1	61	Gunboat	E	$2,500
R-2	61	Cruiser	E	$7,000
R-3	61	Launch	VG	$2,000
R-4	61	Cruiser	E	$8,000
R-5	60	Gunboat	E	$10,000
R-6	61	Pinnace	E	$750
R-7	60	Gunboat	VG	$1,000
Reed, W.S.				
RD-1	27	Battleship	VG	$1,200.
Reil & Co.				
RC-1	160	Liner	E	$1,800
RC-2	157, 160	Paddle-wheeler	E	$900
RC-3	160	Cruiser	E	$900
RC-4	160	Torpedo Boat	E	$900
Richter & Co.				
RR-5	161	Riverboat	E	$800
Robin Toys				
RN-Group	27		G	$25
Rock & Graner				
RG-1	163	Paddle-wheeler	VG	$22,000
RG-2	163	Paddle-wheeler	E	$8,000
RG-3	162	Paddle-wheeler	E	$18,000
RG-4	163	Paddle-wheeler	E	$6,500
Rosenbauer, Karl				
KRN-1	164	Liner	E	$2,500
KRN-2	164	Liner	G	$250
KRN-3	164	Liner	E	$500
Rossignol				
RL-1	62	Gunboat	VG	$150
RL-2	62	Gunboat	E	$1,000
RL-3	62	Speedboat	E	$500
RL-4	62	Gunboat	E	$250
Schieble				
SE-1	28	Gunboat	E	$300
SE-2	28	Battleship	E	$300
SE-3	29	Battleship	E	$900
SE-4	28	Cruiser	E	$1,000

Ref. No.	Page	Type	Cond.	Est. Value	Ref. No.	Page	Type	Cond.	Est. Value
SE-5	29	Battleship	E	$900	ST-17	168	Riverboat	E	$1,500
SE-6	29	Battleship	G	$220	ST-18	168	Riverboat	G	$400
Schoenhut					ST-19	168	Riverboat	G	$250
SC-3	30	Set: Battleship & Sub	VG	$150	ST-20	169	Gunboat	G	$2,000
SC-4	30	Set: Battleship & 2 Subs	VG	$200	ST-21	168	Liner	E	$1,000
Schoenner					**Stereoscopic & Photo Co.**				
SR-1	165	Riverboat	E	$2,500	SPC-1	44	Dingy	E	$450
SR-2	166	Riverboat	VG	$2,500	**Strauss**				
SR-3	165	Riverboat	E	$4,000	SS-1	31	Speedboat	VG	$310
SR-4	165	Battleship	E	$7,000	SS-2	31	Speedboat	E	$150
SR-5	166	Steam Launch	E	$350	SS-3	31	Motorboat w/Dingy	E	$176
Schuco					SS-4	31	Canoe w/Sail	E	$198
SO-1	167	Submarine	E	$100	**Strombeck-Becker**				
SO-2	167	Speedboat	E	$175	STR-1	31	Cruiser	E	$10
SO-3	167	Speedboat	E	$275	STR-2	31	Battleship	E	$10
SO-4	167	Ferry	G	$110	STR-3	31	A/C Carrier	E	$10
Skipper					STR-4	31	Destroyer	E	$10
SK-1	30	Riverboat (Set)	E	$100	STR-5	31	Submarine	E	$10
Spenkuch, Geo.(Nurnberg)					**Sutcliffe**				
SH-1	167	Ships & Sailors	E	$2,000	S-1	46	Liner	E	$150
Star Yacht					S-2	47	Battleship	NM	$350
SY-3	44	Sailboat	E	$192	S-3	46	Submarine	G	$100
Staudt					S-4	46	Submarine	NM	$100
ST-1	169	Gunboat	E	$4,000	S-5	46	Submarine	NM	$100
ST-2	168	Tug	E	$300	S-6	46	Submarine	NM	$100
ST-3	168	Liner	E	$425	S-7	45	Speedboat	E	$750
ST-4	168	Riverboat	P	$250	S-8	45	Speedboat	E	$145
ST-5	168	Riverboat	E	$1,800	S-9	46	Speedboat	E	$150
ST-6	168	Liner	E	$550	S-10	47	Battleship	E	$850
ST-7	169	Battleship	E	$4,000	S-11	45	Pilot Boat	NM	$127
ST-8	169	Gunboat	E	$1,800	S-12	45	Cabin Cruiser	NM	$110
ST-9	170	Speedboat	G	$700	S-13	46	Speedboat	E	$75
ST-10	169	Torpedo Boat	VG	$300	S-14	47	Battleship	E	$850
ST-11	169	Torpedo Boat	VG	$300	S-15	46	Speedboat	E	$150
ST-12	168	Liner	E	$400	S-16	46	Torpedo Boat	E	$150
ST-13	169	Battleship	E	$5,000	S-17	45	Cabin Cruiser	E	$300
ST-14	169	Battleship	E	$2,400	S-18	46	Speedboat	E	$40
ST-15	168	Riverboat	VG	$300	S-19	47	Speedboat	E	$300
ST-16	168	Tug	E	$150	S-20	46	Destroyer	E	$400

Ref. No.	Page	Type	Cond.	Est. Value
Sutcliffe (contd.)				
S-21	45	Speedboat	VG	$250
S-22	46	Gunboat	VG	$93
S-23	47	Speedboat	E	$500
S-24	46	Torpedo Boat	E	$60
Tillicum				
TM-1	32	Battleship	E	$350
TM-2	32	Destroyer	E	$65
TM-3	33	Boat Set #115	E	$160
TM-4	33	Liner	E	$250
TM-5	33	Boat Set T-104	E	$350
TM-6	34	Boat Set T-105	E	$200
TM-7	33	Boat Set T-106	G	$125
TM-8	34	Boat Set T-80	E	$50
TM-9	34	Boat Set T-202	E	$150
TM-10	34	Boat Set T-205	E	$90
TM-11	33	Boat Set T-303	E	$300
TM-12	34	Boat Set T-600	VG	$75
TM-13	34	Boat Set T-630	E	$60
TM-14	32	Freighter	E	$75
TM-15	34	Boat Set T-620	E	$150
TM-16	34	Boat SetT T-610	E	$150
Tootsietoy				
TT-1	35	Navy Set	E	$85
TT-2	35	Convoy Set	VG	$375
TT-3	35	Fleet Set	E	$450
TT-4	35	Navy Set	E	$325
TT-7	35	Boat Set	E	$40
Transogram Co.				
TG-1	35	Boat Blocks	E	$65
Triang				
TR-1	48	Speedboat	E	$75
TR-2	48	Sailboat	E	$200
TR-3	48	Sailboat	G	$150
TR-4	48	Speedboat	E	$100
TR-5	48	Sailboat	E	$115
TR-6	48	Sailboat	E	$300
Trix-Nurnberg				
TX-1	170	Speedboat	E	$150
TX-2	170	Liner	VG	$600
Tudor Button & Novelty				
TBN-1	35	Boat Set	E	$55
TBN-2	35	Boat Set	E	$80
TBN-3	35	Boat Set	VG	$100
Uebelacker				
U-1	172	Paddle-wheeler	VG	$3,500
U-2	173	Rowboat	E	$1,600
U-3	172	Riverboat	E	$4,660
U-4	172	Riverboat	E	$650
U-5	173	Riverboat	G	$6,500
U-6	172	Paddle-wheeler	E	$750
U-8	171	Boat Set	E	$2,000
U-9	171	Boat Set	E	$3,400
U-10	172	Riverboat	G	$600
U-11	172	Gunboat w/2 Towed	E	$1,800
U-12	171	Steam-Sail	F	$300
Union Mfg.Co.				
UN-1	36	Riverboat	E	$5,000
UN-2	36	Riverboat	E	$750
UN-3	36	Riverboat	E	$1,250
Unknown-France				
UK-12	56	Submarine	VG	$1,500
UK-14	63	Submarine	E	$200
UK-41	63	Speedboat	E	$1,500
UK-44	63	Speedboat	E	$300
UK-57	53	Liner-Biscuit Tin	E	$1,200
UK-65	63	Speedboat	E	$500
UK-66	56	Submarine	VG	$1,500
UK-70	53	Liner (Possibly Japanese)	E	$300
UK-78	63	Submarine	E	$600
UK-90	63	Submarine	E	$200
Unknown-Germany				
GZ-1	174	Battle Set	VG	$1,400
UK-1	174	Build-A-Boat	E	$150
UK-4	174	Build-A-Boat	VG	$150
UK-15	125	Liner	E	$150
UK-17	117	Submarine (Made in Japan)	E	$200
UK-18	116	Submarine	F	$200

Ref. No.	Page	Type	Cond.	Est. Value
UK-22	175	Rowboat	VG	$650
UK-24	174	Build-A-Boat	E	$1,540
UK-45	175	Battleship	E	$2,500
UK-46	165	Speedboat	E	$1,000
UK-51	175	Rowboat	G	$1,000
UK-56	112	Liner (Made in Japan)	E	$250
UK-60	101	Tug	E	$1,200
UK-84	163	Paddle-Wheeler	G	$1,000
UK-88	129	Side-Wheeler	E	$1,000
UK-89	166	Riverboat	G	$400

Unknown-UK

Ref. No.	Page	Type	Cond.	Est. Value
UK-67	49	Speedboat	E	$100

Unkown-US

Ref. No.	Page	Type	Cond.	Est. Value
UK-5	3	Build-A-Boat	VG	$150
UK-27	19	Stern-Wheeler	VG	$80
UK-29	20	Speedboat	E	$50
UK-53	20	Speedboat	VG	$15
UK-54	20	Speedboat	VG	$15
UK-64	36	Speedboat	G	$750
UK-96	10	Submarine	E	$25
UK-101	20	Speedboat	E	$165
UK-103	21	Liner	E	$125
UK-104	21	Liner	E	$125

Ventura

Ref. No.	Page	Type	Cond.	Est. Value
VA-1	178	Liner	F	$50
VA-2	177	Liner	E	$2,500
VA-3	178	A/C Carrier	VG	$375
VA-4	178	Heavy Cruiser	E	$2,000
VA-5	178	Cruiser	G	$300
VA-6	178	Aircraft Carrier	E	$475
VA-7	177	Sailboat	E	$750

Walbert

Ref. No.	Page	Type	Cond.	Est. Value
WT-1	36	Sinking Battleship	E	$300
WT-2	36	Ferry	E	$1,815

Weeden

Ref. No.	Page	Type	Cond.	Est. Value
WD-1	37	Launch	VG	$800
WD-2	37	Launch	VG	$800
WD-3	37	Launch	E	$1,200
WD-4	37	Paddle-wheeler	E	$14,000

Wells-Brimtoy

Ref. No.	Page	Type	Cond.	Est. Value
WB-1	49	Paddle-wheeler	E	$160

Wilkins

Ref. No.	Page	Type	Cond.	Est. Value
WK-1	37	Transport	E	$150
WK-2	37	Destroyer	E	$350
WK-3	37	Submarine	E	$200
WK-4	37	Destroyer	NM	$100

Wolverine

Ref. No.	Page	Type	Cond.	Est. Value
W-1	38	Liner	G	$100
W-2	38	Liner	E	$55
W-3	38	Battleship	E	$200
W-4	39	Submarine	E	$125
W-5	39	Submarine	E	$75
W-6	39	Submarine	E	$75
W-7	39	Submarine	E	$75
W-8	39	Submarine	E	$75
W-9	39	Submarine	E	$75
W-10	39	Liner	E	$280
W-11	39	Submarine	E	$200
W-12	38	Liner	E	$175
W-13	38	Aircraft Carrier	VG	$50
W-14	38	Aircraft Carrier	E	$150
W-15	39	Submarine	E	$150
W-16	38	Barge	VG	$25

Wyandotte - All Metal Products Co.

Ref. No.	Page	Type	Cond.	Est. Value
WE-1	39	Liner	E	$95
WE-2	39	Beach Toy	E	$250
WE-3	39	Aircraft Carrier	E	$75
WE-4	39	Liner	G	$30

Bibliography—Books About Toys

Author	Title	Publisher	Date	ISBN
The Hornby Companion Series				
Randall	Vol. 1, The Products of Binns Road	New Cavendish	1977	0-904568-06-
Richardson	Vol. 4, Dinky Toys & Modeled Miniatures	New Cavendish	1981	0-904568-33-4
French	Vol. 4A, Dinky Toy Compendium	New Cavendish	1986	0-904568-85-7
Manduca	Vol. 7, The Meccano Magazine, 1916-1981	New Cavendish	1987	0-904568-37-7
—	Vol. 7A, The Meccano Magazine Anthology	New Cavendish	1991	1-872727-80-8
Beardsley	Vol. 8, The Hornby Companion	New Cavendish	1992	0-904568-95-4
Die Anderen Nürnberger, Technisches Spielzug Aus Der "Guten Alten Zeit":				
Baecker/Haas	Band 1, Bub, Carette, Distler, Doll	Hobby Haas	1973	—
Baecker/Haas	Band 2, Falk, Fleisch, Gunthermann, Kraus, Lehmann	Hobby Haas	1973	—
Baecker/Haas	Band 3, Issmayer, Levy, Plank, Tipp	Hobby Haas	1974	—
Baecker/Haas	Band 4, Einfalt, Klein, Schoenner, Hausmann, A.S.	Hobby Haas	1975	—
Baecker/Haas	Band 5, Arnold, Bub, Carette, Moko, R & Gn, Schuco	Hobby Haas	1976	—
B / Haas / Vaterlein	Band 6, Lehmann, Ullmann & Engelmann, Trix	Hobby Haas	1981	3-86549-1309
B / Jeanmaire / Vaterlein	Band 7, Fleischmann, Staudt, Ullmann & Engelmann	Hobby Haas	1988	3-85649-1317
Märklin, Technical Toys in The Course of Time:				
B / Haas / Jeanmaire	1, 1859-1902	Hastings House	1978	8038-4708-4
B / Haas / Jeanmaire	2, 1904-1908	Hastings House	1978	8038-4704-1
B / Haas / Jeanmaire	4, 1909-1912	Hastings House	1978	8038-4706-8
B / Haas / Jeanmaire	5, 1912-1915	Verlag Eisenbahn	1980	3-85649-105
B / Haas / Jeanmaire	6, 1919-1921	Verlag Eisenbahn	1980	3-85649-106
B / Haas / Jeanmaire	7, 1923-1927	Verlag Eisenbahn	1981	3-85649-107
B / Haas / Jeanmaire	9, 1928-1929	Verlag Eisenbahn	1983	3-85649-109
Baecker / Jeanmaire	11, 1930-1931	Verlag Eisenbahn	1984	3-85649-112
B / Jeanmaire / Vaterlein	12, 1932-1934	Verlag Eisenbahn	1986	3-85649-113-9
B / Jeanmaire / Vaterlein	13, 1935-1936	Verlag Eisenbahn	1989	3-85649-114-7
B / Jeanmaire / Vaterlein	14, 1937-1938	Verlag Eisenbahn	1990	3-85649-115-5
Arick	Toy Boats	Bill Arick		
Arick	Toy Boats	Bill Arick	1993	—
Ayres	The Warner Collector's Guide to American Toys	Warner	1981	0-446-97632-6
Bachmann	The Toy Sample Book of Waldkirchen about 1850	Hastings House	1978	8038-7198-8
Bachmann	German Toys, Der Universal Spielwaren Catalog 1924-1926	Hobby House Press	1985	0-87588-251-X
Baecker / Vaterlein	Vergessenes Blechspielzug	Frank.Fach.Michel.Kohl	1982	—
Baker	Modern Toys, American Toys 1930-1980	Collector Books	1985	0-89145-277-X
Barenholtz	The George Brown Toy Sketchbook	Pyne Press	1971	0-87861-000-6
Barenholtz / McClintock	American Antique Toys, 1830 - 1900	Abrams	1980	0-8109-0668-6
Barlow	The Great American Antique Toy Bazaar, 1879-1945	Windmill Group	1998	0-486-41189-3
Bartholomew	Mechanical Toys	Hamlyn House	1979	0-89009-273-7
Burker / Heard	Pollock's World of Toys	Metcalfe	1975	0-9505588-3-4
Cieslik	Lehmann Toys	New Cavendish	1982	0-904568-40-7

Author	Title	Publisher	Date	ISBN
Cranmer	Cast Iron & Tin Toys of Yesterday	L-W Promotions	1974	–
Culff	The World of Toys	Hamlyn House	1969	600-03872-6
Daiken	Children's Toys Throughout the Ages	Spring Books	1963	–
Doucette / Collins	Collecting Antique Toys, A Pictoral Guide	Macmillan	1981	0-02-533010-1
Duprat	Les Jouets C.R.	Massin	1998	2-7072-0333-5
Favelac	Les Jouets Mechaniques, 1860-1960	Massin	198?	2-7072-0101-4
Fawdry	Pollock's History of English Dolls & Toys	Ernest Benn Ltd.	1979	1-85648-162-X
Fawdry	British Tin Toys	New Cavendish	1990	0-904568-86-5
Flick	Shire Album #147, Old Toys	Shire Pub. Ltd.	1995	0-85263-754-3
Foley	Toys Through The Ages	Chilton	1962	–
Force	Dinky Toys	Schiffer	1988	0-88740-177-5
Franklin	British Biscuit Tins, 1868-1939	New Cavendish	1979	0-904568-11-3
Franzini / Dellanzo	Quel Mondo Dipinto	Editrice Lombarda	1978	–
Franzke	Schuco, Bing & Co.	W. Tummels	1993	3-921590-15-9
Fraser	A History of Toys	Hamlyn House	1972	0-600-34387-1
Freed	Collector's Guide To American Transportation Toys	Freedom	1995	0-9646847-0-5
Freeman	Yesterday's Toys	Century House	1962	–
Freeman	Cavalcade of Toys	Century House	1942	–
Fritzsch/Bachmann	An Illustrated History of German Toys	Hastings House	1978	0-8038-3417-9
Gardiner / Morris	The Illustrated Encyclopedia of Metal Toys	Salamander Books	1984	0-517-55399-6
Gardiner / Morris	The Price Guide To Metal Toys	Antique Collectors' Club	1980	0-902028-92-8
Gardiner / O'Neill	The Collector's All Colour Guide To Transport Toys	Salamander Books	1985	0-86101-205-4
Glaser	Toy Museum Nuremberg	City of N. Toy Museum	1993	–
Guild/Willyard/Konow	Wyandotte Toys Are Good and Safe	Wyandotte Toys Pub.	1996	–
Hanlon	Plastic Toys, Dimestore Dreams of the '40s & '50s	Schiffer	1993	0-88740-460-X
Harley	Shire Album # 248, Construction Toys	Shire Pub. Ltd.	1990	0-7478-0081-2
Harley	Shire Album #193, Toy Boats	Shire Pub. Ltd.	1987	0-85263-851-5
Harley	Toyshop Steam	Argus Books	1978	0-85242-583-X
Harrer	Lexikon Blech Spielzeug	Alba	1989	3-87094-458-7
Head	Bassett-Lowke Waterline Ship Models	New Cavendish	1996	1-872727-72-7
–	Bassett-Lowke (RLYS) Limited- 1902 Catalog	Self	1969	–
Hertz	The Toy Collector	Funk & Wagnals	1969	–
Hertz	Messrs. Ives of Bridgeport	Mark Haber & Co.	1950	–
Hertz	The Handbook of Old American Toys	Mark Haber & Co.	1947	–
Herve	Märklin 1895-1914	Denys Ingram	1983	2-903824-04-5
Hiller	Pagent of Toys	Taplinger	1966	–
Hinrichsen	Spielzeug	Battenberg Verlag	1980	3-87045-177-7
Hirschberg	Steam Toys, A Symphony in Motion	Schiffer	1996	0-7643-0009-1
Holland	More Boys' Toys of The Fifties & Sixties	Windmill Group	1998	1-887790-05-5
Holland/Spong/Whitten	American Live Steam Toys & Their Originators	ATCA	1978	–
Huber	Schuco	Battenberg Verlag	1991	3-89441-236-4

197

Author	Title	Publisher	Date	ISBN
Jaffee	J. Chein & Co. A Collector's Guide To An Am. Toymaker	Schiffer	1997	0-7643-0118-7
Jeanmarie	Nürnberger Spielzeug: Jean Schoenner	Verlag Eisenbahn	1977	3-85649-100-7
Jeanmarie	Bing Metall Spielwaren,1927-32, Archiv NR. 123	Verlag Eisenbahn		3-85649-123-6
Jeanmarie	Gebrüder Bing Im Jugendstil 1909, Archiv NR. 124	Verlag Eisenbahn	1992	3-85649-124-4
Jeanmarie	Deutsches Spielzeug Zur Kriegzeit (1915), NR. 122	Verlag Eisenbahn	1986	3-85649-122-8
Jeanmarie	Gebrüder Bing Spielzeug Zur Vorkriegzeit 1912-15	Verlag Eisenbahn	1977	3-85649-029-9
Jeanmarie	Gebrüder Bing, Die Grossen Nürnberger,1902-1904	Verlag Eisenbahn	1974	3-85649-028
Kaiser / Baecker	Dampfspielzeug	Battenberg Verlag	1993	3-89441-169-4
Kerr	American Tin-Litho Toys	Collector's Press	1995	0-9635202-7-X
Kerr / Gilcher	Ohio Art The World of Toys	Schiffer	1998	0-7643-0512-3
Ketchum	Toys & Games, Cooper-Hewitt Museum	Smithsonian	1981	–
Ketchum	Collecting Toys for Fun and Profit	HP Books	1985	0-89586-250-6
Kihlstrom	Sunday Sailors	Turner	1998	1-56311-467-4
Kimball	Toys, Delights From The Past	Applied Arts	1976	0-911410-40-6
King	A Guide To Metal Toys & Automata	Quintet Pub.	1989	1-85422-3793-9
Lamming / Maeght	Le Jouet De Paris, 1902 - 1968	Arte Adrien Maeght	1988	2-86941-063-8
Lines	Tri-Ang Toys 1937-1938	New Cavendish	1988	0-904568-71-7
Long	Dictionary of Toys Sold In America, Vol. 1	Long	1971	–
Long	Dictionary of Toys Sold In America, Vol. 2	Long	1978	–
Longest	Toys Antique & Collectable	Collector Books	1990	0-89145-402-0
Mackay	Childhood Antiques	Taplinger	1976	0-8008-1442-8
Marsh	Miller's Antiques Checklist,Toys & Games	Reed Int'l	1995	1-85732-273-8
Matthews	Toys Go To War	Pictorial Histories Pub.	1994	0-929521-95-1
McClinton	Antiques of American Childhood	Clarkson N. Potter	1970	–
McCumber	1931 to 1972 Chein Toy and Bank Catalogs	McCumber	1993	–
McGimpsey / Orr	Popular Collectables, Toys	Guinness	1990	0-85112-923-4
Mering & Mestrot	Canots Et Voiliers De Nos Bassins 1935 - 1970	Plein Gaz	2002	2-9519286-0-2
Milet	Les Bateau Jouets	Arte A Paris	1967	–
Milet / Forbes	Toy Boats, 1870-1955, A Pictoral History	Scribner's	1979	0-684-15967-8
Mirken	1927 Edition of The Sears, Roebuck Catalog	Crown	1970	–
Murray	Toys	Studio Vista / Dutton	1968	289-37049-3
Mynheer	Phillips Collectors Guides, Tin Toys	Dunestyle	1988	1-85283-231-2
O'Brien	The Story of American Toys	Cross River Press	1990	0-89659-921-3
O'Neill	The Collectors Encyclopedia of Metal Toys	Crescent	1988	0-517-66531-x
Opie / Alderson	The Treasures of Childhood	Pavillion	1995	1-85793-624-8
Parry-Crooke	Mr. Gamage's Great Toy Bazaar, 1902 -1906	Denys Ingram	1982	8038-47459
Parry-Crooke	Toys Dolls Games, Paris 1903 - 1914	Denys Ingram	1981	8038-7225-9
Perelman	Perelman Antique Toy Museum	Wallace-Homestead	1972	–
Pinsky	Greenberg's Guide To Marx Toys, Volume 1	Greenberg	1988	0-89778-027-2
Pinsky	Greenberg's Guide To Marx Toys, Volume 2	Greenberg	1990	0-89778-1007
Polaine	The War Toys - Kriegsspielzeuge	New Cavendish	1979	0-904568-17-2

Author	Title	Publisher	Date	ISBN
Pressland	Pressland's Great Book of Tin Toys	Golden Age Editions	1995	0-517-02610-7
Pressland	The Art of The Tin Toy	Crown	1976	0-904568-040
Pressland	The Book of Penny Toys	New Cavendish	1991	0-904568-57-7
Ramsay	British Diecast Model Toys	W.S. Cowell	1984	0-9509319-0-X
Remise	Encyclopedie Des Jouets Anciens de 1830-1920, Les Bateaux	Pygmalion / Watelet	1981	2-85704-114-4
Remise	L'Argus Des Jouets Anciens, 1950-1918	Balland	1978	–
Remise / Fondin	The Golden Age of Toys	Edita S.A.	1967	–
Rich	Toys A To Z	Krause	2001	0-87349-240-4
Richardson	The Great Book of Dinky Toys	New Cavendish	2000	1-872727-83-2
Richter	Collector's Guide To Tootsietoys	Collector Books	1991	0-89145-442-X
Robinson	Made In The Ives Shops	Turner	1991	0-938021-83-4
Roulet	Les Dinky Toys Et Dinky Supertoys Francais, 1933-1981	E. P. A.	1984	–
Russell	Christie's Review of The Season 1992	Christie's	1992	0-903432-42-0
Schorr	The Guide To Mehanical Toy Collecting	Performance Media	1982	–
Schroeder	The Wonderful World of Toys, Games & Dolls 1860-1930	Digest	1971	0-695-80219-4
Schwarz	F.A.O. Schwarz Toys Through The Years	Doubleday	1975	0-385-07136-1
Shea	It's All In The Game - A Biography of Milton Bradley	G.P. Putnam's Sons	1960	None
Spero	Toys & Games of The 20'S & 30's From Sears Catalogs	Dover	1988	0-486-258-27-0
Spilhaus	Mechanical Toys	Crown	1989	0-517-56966-3
Swann	The Weeden Manufacturing Co.	Swann	1994	–
Tempest	Collecting Tin Toys	New Cavendish	1994	1-883685-02-8
Tempest	Post-War Tin Toys, A Collector's Guide	Quintet Pub.	1991	0-87069-632-7
Theimer	Au Nain Bleu	Polichinelle	1994	2-9504734-7-4
Vaterlein	Biberacher Blechspielzeug	Betulius	1997	3-89511-013-2
Wagner / Baecker	Blechspielzeug, Schiffe Und Flugkörper	Battenberg Verlag	1991	3-89441-045-0
Walter	Metal Toys From Nuremberg (Kellermann 1910-1979)	Schiffer	1992	0-88740-435-9
Weltens	Mechanical Tin Toys in Colour	Blanford Press	1977	0-7137-0848-4
White	Antique Toys	Chancellor Press	1971	0-907486-22-3
White	Toys & Dolls Marks & Labels	Branford	1975	0-8231-3031-0
Whitton	American Clockwork Toys 1862 -1900	Schiffer	1981	0916839-55-2
Whitton	Knopf Collectors' Guides, Toys	Knopf	1984	0-394-71526-8
Whitton	Bliss Toys and Dollhouses	Dover	1979	0-486-23790-7
Wieland / Force	Tootsietoys, The World's First Diecast Models	MotorBooks Int'l	1980	0-87938-065-9
–	The Great Toys of Georges Carette, 1911, 1905, 1914	New Cavendish	1979	0-904568-02-4
–	The 1898 Bing Toy Catalog	New Cavendish	1991	1-872727-70-0
–	The 1906 Bing Toy Catalog, Including 1907 Supp.	New Cavendish	1991	0-904568-52-0
–	The 1912 Bing Toy Catalogue Includ. Plush & Felt	New Cavendish	2001	1-872727-75-1
–	Die Welt Aus Blech	Phillip Von Zabern	1981	3-8053-0529-x
–	Made for N.Y. The Lawrence Scripps Wilkinson Coll.	NY Historical Society	1986	–
–	Spielzeug Museum Trier	Spielzeug Museum Trier	1990	–

Toy Catalogs

Distributor or Manufacturer	Date	Distributor or Manufacturer	Date	Distributor or Manufacturer	Date
Althof, Bergman	1874	F.A.O. Schwarz	1952	Märklin	1938/39
American Made Toys	1918	F.A.O. Schwarz	1953	Meccano	1937
American National	1923	F.A.O. Schwarz	1954	Meccano	1938
Basset-Lowke	1938	F.A.O. Schwarz	1955	Meccano	1938-9
Basset-Lowke	1938	F.A.O. Schwarz	1956	Milton Bradley	1950'S
Basset-Lowke	1940	F.A.O. Schwarz	1956	Milton Bradley	1948
Basset-Lowke	1939	F.A.O. Schwarz	1957	Milton Bradley	1949
Bing	1915	F.A.O. Schwarz	1957	Milton Bradley	1953
Bing	1915	F.A.O. Schwarz	1958	Montgomery Ward	1954
Bing	1928	F.A.O. Schwarz	1958	Orkin	1920
Bliss	1889	F.A.O. Schwarz	1959	Orkin Craft	1930'S
Bliss	1896	F.A.O. Schwarz	1960	Paya Linea Historica	1985
Bonnet, Victor	191?	F.A.O. Schwarz	1960	Plank	1903
Boucher	1921	F.A.O. Schwarz	1962	Schoenhut	1915
Boucher	1922	F.A.O. Schwarz	1963	Schoenhut	1926
Boucher	1923	Heller, Coudray et Cie	1900	Schoenhut	1928
Boucher	1928	Horsman, E.I.	1892	Scott Mfg. Co.	1924
Boucher	1951	Ives	1918	Sears	1900
Carette	1911	Ives	1918	Sears	1927
Carette	1911	Ives	1920	Staudt, Georg L.	1888
Carette	1910 ?	Ives	1921	Stevens & Brown	1872
Cass, N.D.	1929	Ives	1922	Strassburger	1880
Cohn, T. ,Inc.	1959	Ives	1922	Strauss, Ferdinand	1925
Converse	1912	Ives	1923	Strauss, Ferdinand	1926
Converse	1913	Ives	1925	Strauss, Jos. Buffalo	193?
Converse	1927	Ives	1926	Supplee-Biddle	1930
Dayton	1929	Ives	1926	N. Sure Co.,Chicago	1935
Dent Hardware	1910	Ives	1927	Tillicum	1930
Dent Hardware	191?	Ives	1927	Tryon, E.K.,Co.	1935
Dent Hardware	192?	Ives	1918	Walbert	1930
Dent Hardware	192?	Ives	1918	Wilkins Toy Co.	1895
F.A.O. Schwarz	1906-7	Ives	1918	Wilkins Toy Co.	1911
F.A.O. Schwarz	1917	Ives	1922	Wolverine	193?
F.A.O. Schwarz	1918	Keystone	1922	Wolverine	193?
F.A.O. Schwarz	1919	Keystone	1925	Wolverine	1927
F.A.O. Schwarz	1921-22	Keystone	1933	Wolverine	1958
F.A.O. Schwarz	1926	Kingsbury	1929-30	Wolverine	1959
F.A.O. Schwarz	1927	Kingsbury	1931		
F.A.O. Schwarz	1947	Lionel	1935-39		
F.A.O. Schwarz	1950	Märklin	1930		
F.A.O. Schwarz	1951	Märklin	1934/35		

Related Reading - Maritime

Author	Title	Publisher	Date	L. of Congress or ISBN
Liners				
Adams	Ocean Steamers	New Cavendish	1993	0-904568-89-X
Ballard & Archbold	Lost Liners	Hyperion	1997	0-7868-6296-3
Blair & Ansel	Chesapeake Bay Notes & Sketches	Tidewater	1981	0-807033-277-5
Bonsall	Great Shipwrecks of The 20th Century	Bookman	1988	0-8317-7781-8
Braynard	The World's Greatest Ship, Leviathan, Vol 1	S.St.Seaport Mus.	1972	(LC) 72-85207
Braynard	The World's Greatest Ship, Leviathan, Vol 2	S.St.Seaport Mus.	1974	(LC) 72-85207
Braynard	The World's Greatest Ship, Leviathan, Vol 3	S.St.Seaport Mus.	1976	(LC) 72-85207
Braynard	The World's Greatest Ship, Leviathan, Vol 4	Mariner's Museum	1972	(LC) 72-85207
Braynard	The World's Greatest Ship, Leviathan, Vol 5	(Private)	1981	(LC) 72-85207
Braynard	The World's Greatest Ship, Leviathan, Vol 6	Am.M.M Academy	–	0-96-06204-5-1
Braynard	The Big Ship, The Story of The SS United States	Mariner's Museum	1981	0-9117376-37-4
Braynard & Miller	Fifty Famous Liners, Vol.1	Norton	1982	0-393-01611-0
Braynard & Miller	Fifty Famous Liners, Vol.2	Norton	1985	0-393-01947-0
Braynard & Miller	Fifty Famous Liners, Vol.3	Norton	1987	0-393-02551-9
Butler	Lusitania	Random House	1982	0-394-52809-3
Cairis	Passenger Liners of The World Since 1893	Bonanza	1979	0-517-28875-3
Cox	Paddle Steamers	Blandford Press	1979	0-7137-024-3
Dunn	Merchantships of The World 1910-29	Macmillan	1975	–
Griffin	Paddle Steamers	Hugh Evelyn	1968	238-78888-1
Holly	Tidewater By Steamboat	Johns Hopkins	1991	0-8018-4168-2
Hughs	The Blue Riband of The Atlantic	Scribner's Sons	1973	0-684-13777-1
Isherwood	Cunard Portraits	World Ship Soc.	1990	0-905617-57-6
Kludas	Great Passenger Ships of The World, Vol I	Stephens	1975	0-85059-174-0
Kludas	Great Passenger Ships of The World, Vol 2	Stephens	1976	0-85059-242-9
Kludas	Great Passenger Ships of The World, Vol 3	Stephens	1976	0-85059-245-3
Kludas	Great Passenger Ships of The World, Vol 4	Stephens	1977	0-85059-253-4
Kludas	Great Passenger Ships of The World, Vol 5	Stephens	1977	0-85059-265-8
Kludas	Great Passenger Ships of The World, Vol 6	Stephens	1986	0-85059-747-1
Le Huede	Dining on The France	Vendome	1981	0-86565-013-6
Lord	A Night To Remember	Henry Holt	1956	(LC) 55-10643
Lord	The Night Lives On	Morrow	1986	0-688-04939-7
Maddocks	The Seafarers, The Great Liners	Time-Life	1978	0-8094-2664-1
Maxtone-Graham	Liners To The Sun	Macmillan	1985	0-02-545010-7
Maxtone-Graham	The Only Way To Cross	Macmillan	1978	0-02-096010-7
Miller	SS Independence, SS Constitution	Purple Mt. Press	2001	(LC) 2001012345

Related Reading - Maritime (contd.)

Author	Title	Publisher	Date	L. of Congress or ISBN
Miller	The Last Atlantic Liners	Conway	1985	0-312-46971-3
Moscow	Collision Course	Grosset & Dunlap	1981	0-448-12019-4
Newell	Ocean Liners of The 20th Century	Bonanza	1963	(LC) 63-18494
Rentell	Historic White Star Liners	Blue Water Pub.	1987	0-9512313-0-8
Schaap & Schaap	A Bridge To The Seven Seas	Stephens	1973	0-85059-127-9
Server	The Golden Age of Ocean Liners	Todtri Production	1996	1-880908-86-7
Simpson	The Lusitania	Little-Brown	1973	0-316-79178-4
Thomas & Morgan-Witts	The Strange Fate of The Morrow Castle	Collins	1973	0-00-211743-6
Turner	The Pacific Princesses	Sono Nis Press	1977	0-919462-04-9
Wall	Ocean Liners	Dutton & Co	1977	0-525-16990-3
Warren	The Mauretania	Stephens	1987	0-85059-914-8
Warren	The Shipbuilder 1906-1914, Volume 1	Blue Riband Pub	1995	0-9648153-0-3
Warren	TheShipbuilder 1907-1914, Volume 2	Blue Riband Pub	1995	0-9648153-1-1
Warwick	QE2	Norton	1993	0-393-03547-6
Williams & Kerbrech	Damned By Destiny	Teredo Books	1982	0-903662-09-4
–	Ocean Liners of The Past, Olympic & Titanic	Stephens	1976	0-85059-046-9
–	Ocean Liners of The Past, Lusitania Mauritania	Stephens	1970	0-85059-054-X
–	Ocean Liners of The Past, Aquitania	Stephens	1971	0-85059-070-1

Submarines

Author	Title	Publisher	Date	L. of Congress or ISBN
Blair	Silent Victory Volume 1	Lippincott	1975	–
Blair	Silent Victory Volume 2	Lippincott	1975	–
Blair	Hitler's U-Boat War, The Hunters 1939-42	Random House	1996	0-394-58839-8
Botting	The Seafarers, The U-Boats	Time-Life	1979	0-8094-2675-7
Edwards	The Twilight of The U-Boats	Naval Inst. Press	2004	1-59114-884-7
Everitt	K Boats	Naval Inst. Press	1963	1-55750-467-9
Friedman	U.S. Submarines Through 1945	Naval Inst. Press	1995	1-55750-263-3
Gannon	Black May	Harper Collins	1989	0-06-017819-1
Hoyt	U Boats, A Pictorial History	Mcgraw Hill	1987	0-07-030620-6
Kemp	U-Boats Destroyed	Naval Inst. Press	1997	1-55750-847-X
Konig	Voyage of The Deutschland	Naval Inst. Press	2001	1-55750-424-5
Maas	The Terrible Hours	Harper Collins	1999	0-06-019480-4
Mason	U-Boat, The Secret Menace	Ballentine Books	1968	–
Mulligan	Neither Sharks Nor Wolves	Naval Inst. Press	1999	1-55750-594-2
Sasgen	Red Scorpion	Naval Inst. Press	2002	1-55750-404-0
Schaeffer	U-Boat 977	Norton	1953	–
Sontag & Drew	Blind Man's Bluff	Public Affairs	1998	1-891620-08-8

Author	Title	Publisher	Date	L.of Congress or ISBN
Thomas	Raiders of The Deep	Doubleday	1928	–
Thornton	Submarine Insignia	Naval Inst. Press	1997	1-5570-843-7
Vause	Wolf	Naval Inst. Press	1997	1-5570-874-7
Werner	Iron Coffins	Holt, Rinehart	1969	–
Wiggins	U-Boat Adventures	Naval Inst. Press	1999	1-5570-950-6

Warships Other Than Sail

Author	Title	Publisher	Date	L.of Congress or ISBN
Ballard	Return To Midway	Nat'l Geographic	1999	0-7922-7500-4
Beach	Wreck of The Memphis	Naval Inst. Press	1966	1-55750-070-3
Bearss	Hardluck Ironclad	LSU Press	1985	0-8071-0683-6
Bridgland	Sea Killers In Disguise	Naval Inst. Press	1999	1-55750-895-X
Conway (Editors)	All The World's Fighting Ships 1860-1905	Conway Mar. Press	2002	0-85177-133-5
Conway (Editors)	All The World's Fighting Ships 1906-1921	Conway Mar. Press	2002	0-85177-245-5
Cutler	The Battle of Leyte Gulf	Naval Inst. Press	1994	1-55750-243-9
Evans	Building The Steam Navy	Conway Mar. Press	2004	0-85177-959-X
Fleming	Warships of World War I	Ian Allan	1967	–
Fraccaroli	Italian Warships of World War II	Ian Allan	1968	–
Friedman	U.S. Battleships	Naval Inst. Press	1985	0-87021-715-1
Gleichauf	Unsung Sailors	Naval Inst. Press	2002	1-55750-420-2
Galuppini	Warships of The World	Military Press	1986	0-517-68252-4
Gray	Hitler's Battleships	Naval Inst. Press	1999	1-55750-343-5
Groner	German Warships 1815-1945, Volume 1	Naval Inst. Press	1990	0-87021-790-9
Hailey & Lancelot	Clear For Action	Bonanza	1964	–
Hewson	The WW II Warship Guide	Chartwell Books	2000	0-7858-1230-X
Hill	The Oxford Ill. Hist. of The Royal Navy	Oxford U. Press	1995	0-19-211675-4
Hoehling	The Lexington Goes Down	Prentice-Hall	1971	0-13-535252-5
Hough	The Great Dreadnought	Harper & Row	1967	–
Hough	Dreadnought	Macmillan	1964	–
Howarth	The Seafarers, The Dreadnoughts	Time-Life	1979	0-8094-2723-3
Hoyt	Kreuzerkrieg	World Pub.	1968	(LC)67-24477
Hythe	The Naval Annual 1913	Arco	1970	(LC) 76-108346
Irving	The Smoke Screen of Jutland	Mckay	1967	–
Jane	Jane's Fighting Ships 1905 / 6	Arco	1969	668-02269-8
Jane	Jane's Fighting Ships 1906 / 7	Arco	1970	668-02019-9
Jane	Jane's Fighting Ships 1914	Arco	1969	668-01873-9
Johnston	Queen of The Flat-Tops	Dutton & Co	1942	–
Kemp	Convoy - Drama In Arctic Waters	Cassell & Co	1993	0-304-35451-1
Koenig	Epic Sea Battles	Chartwell Books	1975	0-7064-0445-9
Lenton & Colledge	Warships of World War II	Ian Allan	1968	–

Related Reading - Maritime (contd.)

Author	Title	Publisher	Date	L. of Congress or ISBN
Lochner	The Last Gentleman of War (Emden)	Naval Inst. Press	2002	1-55750-538-1
Lord	Lonely Vigil	Viking Press	1977	0-670-43765-4
Lord	Day of Infamy	Henry Holt	1957	(LC) 57-6189
Lord	Incredible Victory	Harper & Row	1967	(LC) 67-13687
Macintyre	The Naval War Against Hitler	Scribner's Sons	1971	—
Madsen	Forgotten Fleet - The Mothball Navy	Naval Inst. Press	1999	1-55750-543-8
Madsen	Resurrection	Naval Inst. Press	2003	1-55750-488-1
Mehl	Naval Guns - 500 Yrs of Ship & Coastal Artillery	Naval Inst. Press	2002	1-59114-557-0
Morison	The Two Ocean War	Little-Brown	1963	(LC) 63-8307
Mullenheim-Rechberg	Battleship Bismarck	Naval Inst. Press	2002	1-55750-436-9
Newell & Smith	Mighty Mo	Bonanza	1969	—
Padfield	The Battleship Era	Mckay	1972	(LC) 72-89388
Padfield	Guns At Sea	St. Martin's Press	1974	—
Pater	United States Battleships	Monitor	1968	—
Polmar	Guide To The Soviet Navy, Third Edition	Naval Inst. Press	1984	—
Potter	Fiasco	Stein and Day	1970	8128-1276-X
Preston	Battleships 1856-1977	Chartwell Books	1977	0-89009-126-9
Preston	Cruisers	Bison	1982	0-86124-064-2
Reckner	Teddy Roosevelt's Great White Fleet	Naval Inst. Press	2001	1-55750-972-7
Regan	The Guinness Book of Naval Blunders	Guinness	1994	0-85112-713-4
Rodgers	Naval Warfare Under Oars	Naval Inst. Press	1940	0-87021-487-X
Ropp	Development of A Modern Navy-French 1871-1904	Naval Inst. Press	1987	0-87021-141-2
Roscoe & Freeman	Picture History of The U.S. Navy	Bonanza	1956	—
Shirer	The Sinking of The Bismarck	Random House	1962	—
Silverstone	U.S. Warships of World War II	Doubleday	—	—
Silverstone	U.S. Warships of World War I	Doubleday	1970	(LC) 71-111291
Stewart	The Battle of Leyte Gulf	Robert Hale	1979	0-7091-7544-2
Still, Taylor, Delany	Raiders and Blockaders	Brassey's	1998	1-57488-238-4
Taylor	German Warships of World War II	Doubleday	1967	—
Thomas	Count Luckner, The Sea Devil	Doubleday	1928	—
Tute	The Deadly Stroke	Coward, Mccann	1973	698-10501-X
Warner	Great Sea Battles	Spring	1968	—
Watts	Japanese Warships of WW II	Doubleday	1967	—
White	They Were Expendable	Harcourt, Brace	1942	—
Williams	Naval Camouflage 1914-1945	Naval Inst. Press	2001	1-55750-496-2
—	The Encyclopedia of Sea Warfare	Crowell	1975	0-690-00769-8
—	Sea Power	Exeter	1979	0-89637-011-5

PRINCE OF WALES